TEACHER'S PET PUBLICATIONS

PUZZLE PACK
for
Number the Stars

based on the book by
Lois Lowry

Written by
William T. Collins

© 2005 Teacher's Pet Publications
All Rights Reserved

The materials in this packet are copyrighted
by Teacher's Pet Publications, Inc.

These pages may be duplicated by the purchaser
for use in the purchaser's own classroom.

Copying any of these materials and distributing them
for any other purpose is a violation of the copyright laws.

© 2005 Teacher's Pet Publications, Inc.
www.tpet.com

INTRODUCTION
If you already own the LitPlan for this title, this Puzzle Pack will refresh your Unit Resource Materials and Vocabulary Resource Materials sections plus give you additional materials you can substitute into the tests. If you do not already have a complete LitPlan, these pages will give you some supplemental materials to use with your own plan. There are two main groups of materials: one set for unit words (such as characters' names, symbols, places, etc.) and one set for vocabulary words associated with the book.

WORD LIST
There is a word list for both the unit words and the vocabulary words. These lists show you which words are being used in the materials and the clues or definitions being used for those words. You may want to give students a word list with clues/definitions to help them, or you may want students to only have a word list (without clues/definitions) if you want them to work a little harder. Both are available for duplication. The word lists can also be your "calling key" for the bingo games.

FILL IN THE BLANK AND MATCHING
There are 4 each of the fill in the blank and matching worksheets for both the unit and vocabulary words. These pages can be used either as extra worksheets for students or as objective parts of a unit test. They can be done individually if students need extra help or as a whole class activity to review the material covered.

MAGIC SQUARES
The magic squares not only reinforce the material covered but also work on reasoning and math skills. Many teachers have told us that their students really enjoy doing these!

WORD SEARCH PUZZLES
The word search words go in all directions, as indicated on your answer keys. Two of the word search puzzles have the clues listed rather than the words. This makes the puzzle a little more difficult, but it reinforces the material better. Two word search puzzles have words only for students who find the clue puzzles too difficult.

CROSSWORD PUZZLES
Both unit and vocabulary word sections have 4 crossword puzzles.

BINGO CARDS
There are 32 individual bingo cards for the unit words and 32 individual bingo cards for the vocabulary words. You can use your word list as a "call list," calling the words at random and marking them off of your list as you go, or you could use the flash cards by cutting them apart and drawing the words at random from a hat (or box or whatever). To make a better review, you might ask for the definition and spelling of each word as you call it out–or you could call out the definitions and have students tell you the words they need to look for on the puzzle.

JUGGLE LETTERS
The vocabulary juggle letter game is intended to help students learn the spellings of the words. One sheet has the definitions listed on it as an extra help for students who need it or to reinforce the definitions if you choose to do so.

FLASH CARDS
We've included a set of vocabulary flash cards you can duplicate, cut, and fold for your students. Some teachers make a few sets for general use by the class; others make a set for each student. Some teachers duplicate them for each student and have the students cut & fold their own. You can cut out just the words and put them in a hat, have each student pick out one word and write the definition and a sentence for that word. Students then swap words and papers, with the next student adding a sentence of his own under the last one. You can have students swap as many times as you like. Each time the student will read the sentences written prior to his own and then add a sentence. You can cut out the words and definitions separately and play "I Have; Who Has?" Each student in the room draws a word and definition. The first student says, "I have (the name of the word). Who has the definition?" The student with the definition reads it then says, "I have (the name of the vocabulary word she has). Who has the definition?" The round continues until all words and definitions have been given.

Number the Stars Unit Word List

No.	Word	Clue/Definition
1.	AMALIENBORG	Copenhagen palace
2.	ANDERSON	Danish fairy tale author, Hans Christian _____
3.	ANNEMARIE	Courageous young Danish girl
4.	BALTIC	Borders Denmark to the east, _____ Sea
5.	BIRTE	Pretend dead aunt
6.	BLOSSOM	Provided family with milk
7.	BODYGUARD	All of Denmark is King Christian's
8.	CHRISTIAN	Danish king, _____ the tenth
9.	COFFIN	Hid blankets and clothes
10.	COPENHAGEN	Capital of Denmark
11.	CROCHETING	Mrs. Johansen did this the night Lise was killed
12.	CUPCAKES	Pink frosted ones were nowhere to be found
13.	DANSKE	De Frie _____
14.	DENMARK	Setting
15.	DRESS	Lise danced in it on her engagement, yellow _____
16.	DRUNKARD	How Mama looked when she broke her ankle
17.	ELLEN	Jewish friend of Annemarie
18.	FIREWORKS	Explosion of Danish naval fleet on Kirsti's bday
19.	FISH SHOES	Kirsti refused to wear
20.	FUNERAL	Trick to fool Nazis
21.	GARDENS	Copenhagen fun spot, Tivoli _____
22.	GILLELEJE	Coast of Denmark near Sweden
23.	GIRAFFE	Nickname for tall Nazi soldier
24.	GONE	Mama's favorite story, _____ With The Wind
25.	HANDKERCHIEF	Delivered by Annemarie to Henrik
26.	HENRIK	Fisherman who lives by the sea, Uncle _____
27.	HIRSH	Button shop lady, Mrs. _____
28.	HOLOCAUST	Persecution of Jews by Nazis
29.	INGEBORG	Smuggled Jews out of Denmark
30.	JUBILEE	King Christian's faithful horse
31.	KATTEGAT	North Sea channel between Sweden and Denmark
32.	KIRSTI	Obstinate younger sister of Annemarie
33.	KRONER	Danish money
34.	LEATHER	None is available during war
35.	LISE	Older sister of Annemarie and Kirsti
36.	LOWRY	Author
37.	NORTH	Borders Denmark to the west, _____ Sea
38.	OCCUPATION	Nazi soldiers patrolling in Denmark, Nazi _____
39.	OSTERBROGADE	Copenhagen street
40.	PETER	Red-headed fiance of Lise
41.	PHOTOGRAPH	Used to prevent Ellen's detection
42.	PRIDE	Strong Jewish trait
43.	PSALM	Contains words in title of book
44.	RESISTANCE	Worked secretly against Nazis
45.	ROSEN	Jewish schoolteacher, Mr. _____
46.	RUCKSACK	Girls' bookbag
47.	SEASICK	How Mrs. Rosen felt in the boat
48.	SLAPPED	Nazi soldier did this to Mama
49.	SPECIAL	Once you're greeted by a king
50.	STAR	Symbol of Jewish faith, _____ of David
51.	SWASTIKA	Nazi symbol
52.	SWEDEN	Jews were taken to this place by boat
53.	THUNDER	Kirsti's kitten; God of _____

Number the Stars Unit Word List

No.	Word	Clue/Definition
54.	TROFAST	Fatihful dog of Mama's
55.	TRUNK	Lise's trousseau is in it
56.	TYPHUS	Cause of Great Aunt Birte's death

Number the Stars Fill In The Blank 1

_____ 1. North Sea channel between Sweden and Denmark

_____ 2. Worked secretly against Nazis

_____ 3. Mama's favorite story, _____ With The Wind

_____ 4. De Frie _____

_____ 5. How Mrs. Rosen felt in the boat

_____ 6. Lise's trousseau is in it

_____ 7. Jews were taken to this place by boat

_____ 8. Strong Jewish trait

_____ 9. Contains words in title of book

_____ 10. Provided family with milk

_____ 11. Explosion of Danish naval fleet on Kirsti's bday

_____ 12. Pink frosted ones were nowhere to be found

_____ 13. Copenhagen street

_____ 14. Author

_____ 15. Jewish schoolteacher, Mr. _____

_____ 16. Kirsti's kitten; God of _____

_____ 17. Setting

_____ 18. Mrs. Johansen did this the night Lise was killed

_____ 19. Obstinate younger sister of Annemarie

_____ 20. Coast of Denmark near Sweden

Number the Stars Fill In The Blank 1 Answer Key

KATTEGAT	1. North Sea channel between Sweden and Denmark
RESISTANCE	2. Worked secretly against Nazis
GONE	3. Mama's favorite story, _____ With The Wind
DANSKE	4. De Frie _____
SEASICK	5. How Mrs. Rosen felt in the boat
TRUNK	6. Lise's trousseau is in it
SWEDEN	7. Jews were taken to this place by boat
PRIDE	8. Strong Jewish trait
PSALM	9. Contains words in title of book
BLOSSOM	10. Provided family with milk
FIREWORKS	11. Explosion of Danish naval fleet on Kirsti's bday
CUPCAKES	12. Pink frosted ones were nowhere to be found
OSTERBROGADE	13. Copenhagen street
LOWRY	14. Author
ROSEN	15. Jewish schoolteacher, Mr. _____
THUNDER	16. Kirsti's kitten; God of _____
DENMARK	17. Setting
CROCHETING	18. Mrs. Johansen did this the night Lise was killed
KIRSTI	19. Obstinate younger sister of Annemarie
GILLELEJE	20. Coast of Denmark near Sweden

Number the Stars Fill In The Blank 2

_____ 1. Used to prevent Ellen's detection

_____ 2. Button shop lady, Mrs. _____

_____ 3. Nickname for tall Nazi soldier

_____ 4. Worked secretly against Nazis

_____ 5. None is available during war

_____ 6. Danish money

_____ 7. Coast of Denmark near Sweden

_____ 8. Nazi soldier did this to Mama

_____ 9. Mrs. Johansen did this the night Lise was killed

_____ 10. North Sea channel between Sweden and Denmark

_____ 11. Borders Denmark to the west, _____ Sea

_____ 12. Red-headed fiance of Lise

_____ 13. Kirsti's kitten; God of _____

_____ 14. Lise's trousseau is in it

_____ 15. Mama's favorite story, _____ With The Wind

_____ 16. Explosion of Danish naval fleet on Kirsti's bday

_____ 17. Jews were taken to this place by boat

_____ 18. Pretend dead aunt

_____ 19. Fisherman who lives by the sea, Uncle _____

_____ 20. Persecution of Jews by Nazis

Number the Stars Fill In The Blank 2 Answer Key

PHOTOGRAPH	1.	Used to prevent Ellen's detection
HIRSH	2.	Button shop lady, Mrs. _____
GIRAFFE	3.	Nickname for tall Nazi soldier
RESISTANCE	4.	Worked secretly against Nazis
LEATHER	5.	None is available during war
KRONER	6.	Danish money
GILLELEJE	7.	Coast of Denmark near Sweden
SLAPPED	8.	Nazi soldier did this to Mama
CROCHETING	9.	Mrs. Johansen did this the night Lise was killed
KATTEGAT	10.	North Sea channel between Sweden and Denmark
NORTH	11.	Borders Denmark to the west, _____ Sea
PETER	12.	Red-headed fiance of Lise
THUNDER	13.	Kirsti's kitten; God of _____
TRUNK	14.	Lise's trousseau is in it
GONE	15.	Mama's favorite story, _____ With The Wind
FIREWORKS	16.	Explosion of Danish naval fleet on Kirsti's bday
SWEDEN	17.	Jews were taken to this place by boat
BIRTE	18.	Pretend dead aunt
HENRIK	19.	Fisherman who lives by the sea, Uncle _____
HOLOCAUST	20.	Persecution of Jews by Nazis

Number the Stars Fill In The Blank 3

_____ 1. Capital of Denmark

_____ 2. Nickname for tall Nazi soldier

_____ 3. Once you're greeted by a king

_____ 4. Danish money

_____ 5. Copenhagen palace

_____ 6. Provided family with milk

_____ 7. Copenhagen fun spot, Tivoli _____

_____ 8. De Frie _____

_____ 9. Author

_____ 10. Jews were taken to this place by boat

_____ 11. How Mrs. Rosen felt in the boat

_____ 12. Girls' bookbag

_____ 13. Worked secretly against Nazis

_____ 14. Hid blankets and clothes

_____ 15. None is available during war

_____ 16. Persecution of Jews by Nazis

_____ 17. Strong Jewish trait

_____ 18. Trick to fool Nazis

_____ 19. Symbol of Jewish faith, _____ of David

_____ 20. Jewish schoolteacher, Mr. _____

Number the Stars Fill In The Blank 3 Answer Key

COPENHAGEN	1. Capital of Denmark
GIRAFFE	2. Nickname for tall Nazi soldier
SPECIAL	3. Once you're greeted by a king
KRONER	4. Danish money
AMALIENBORG	5. Copenhagen palace
BLOSSOM	6. Provided family with milk
GARDENS	7. Copenhagen fun spot, Tivoli _____
DANSKE	8. De Frie _____
LOWRY	9. Author
SWEDEN	10. Jews were taken to this place by boat
SEASICK	11. How Mrs. Rosen felt in the boat
RUCKSACK	12. Girls' bookbag
RESISTANCE	13. Worked secretly against Nazis
COFFIN	14. Hid blankets and clothes
LEATHER	15. None is available during war
HOLOCAUST	16. Persecution of Jews by Nazis
PRIDE	17. Strong Jewish trait
FUNERAL	18. Trick to fool Nazis
STAR	19. Symbol of Jewish faith, _____ of David
ROSEN	20. Jewish schoolteacher, Mr. _____

Number the Stars Fill In The Blank 4

_____ 1. Older sister of Annemarie and Kirsti

_____ 2. Contains words in title of book

_____ 3. Pink frosted ones were nowhere to be found

_____ 4. Hid blankets and clothes

_____ 5. Nickname for tall Nazi soldier

_____ 6. Jewish friend of Annemarie

_____ 7. How Mrs. Rosen felt in the boat

_____ 8. Used to prevent Ellen's detection

_____ 9. Capital of Denmark

_____ 10. Persecution of Jews by Nazis

_____ 11. Delivered by Annemarie to Henrik

_____ 12. Kirsti's kitten; God of _____

_____ 13. Mama's favorite story, _____ With The Wind

_____ 14. Copenhagen street

_____ 15. Worked secretly against Nazis

_____ 16. Copenhagen fun spot, Tivoli _____

_____ 17. Fisherman who lives by the sea, Uncle _____

_____ 18. Mrs. Johansen did this the night Lise was killed

_____ 19. All of Denmark is King Christian's

_____ 20. Smuggled Jews out of Denmark

Number the Stars Fill In The Blank 4 Answer Key

LISE	1. Older sister of Annemarie and Kirsti
PSALM	2. Contains words in title of book
CUPCAKES	3. Pink frosted ones were nowhere to be found
COFFIN	4. Hid blankets and clothes
GIRAFFE	5. Nickname for tall Nazi soldier
ELLEN	6. Jewish friend of Annemarie
SEASICK	7. How Mrs. Rosen felt in the boat
PHOTOGRAPH	8. Used to prevent Ellen's detection
COPENHAGEN	9. Capital of Denmark
HOLOCAUST	10. Persecution of Jews by Nazis
HANDKERCHIEF	11. Delivered by Annemarie to Henrik
THUNDER	12. Kirsti's kitten; God of _____
GONE	13. Mama's favorite story, _____ With The Wind
OSTERBROGADE	14. Copenhagen street
RESISTANCE	15. Worked secretly against Nazis
GARDENS	16. Copenhagen fun spot, Tivoli _____
HENRIK	17. Fisherman who lives by the sea, Uncle _____
CROCHETING	18. Mrs. Johansen did this the night Lise was killed
BODYGUARD	19. All of Denmark is King Christian's
INGEBORG	20. Smuggled Jews out of Denmark

Number the Stars Matching 1

___ 1. FUNERAL   A. Smuggled Jews out of Denmark
___ 2. DRUNKARD   B. Contains words in title of book
___ 3. GARDENS   C. Borders Denmark to the east, _____ Sea
___ 4. KRONER   D. De Frie _____
___ 5. SWASTIKA   E. Lise's trousseau is in it
___ 6. INGEBORG   F. Worked secretly against Nazis
___ 7. HIRSH   G. Pretend dead aunt
___ 8. BODYGUARD   H. Fatiful dog of Mama's
___ 9. FIREWORKS   I. Delivered by Annemarie to Henrik
___10. HANDKERCHIEF   J. Coast of Denmark near Sweden
___11. TROFAST   K. Used to prevent Ellen's detection
___12. PHOTOGRAPH   L. Button shop lady, Mrs. _____
___13. DANSKE   M. Trick to fool Nazis
___14. OCCUPATION   N. Nazi symbol
___15. HOLOCAUST   O. Danish money
___16. CUPCAKES   P. Cause of Great Aunt Birte's death
___17. BALTIC   Q. Borders Denmark to the west, _____ Sea
___18. RESISTANCE   R. How Mama looked when she broke her ankle
___19. BIRTE   S. Kirsti's kitten; God of _____
___20. TYPHUS   T. All of Denmark is King Christian's
___21. TRUNK   U. Persecution of Jews by Nazis
___22. PSALM   V. Nazi soldiers patrolling in Denmark, Nazi _____
___23. NORTH   W. Copenhagen fun spot, Tivoli _____
___24. GILLELEJE   X. Pink frosted ones were nowhere to be found
___25. THUNDER   Y. Explosion of Danish naval fleet on Kirsti's bday

Number the Stars Matching 1 Answer Key

M - 1. FUNERAL	A.	Smuggled Jews out of Denmark
R - 2. DRUNKARD	B.	Contains words in title of book
W - 3. GARDENS	C.	Borders Denmark to the east, _____ Sea
O - 4. KRONER	D.	De Frie _____
N - 5. SWASTIKA	E.	Lise's trousseau is in it
A - 6. INGEBORG	F.	Worked secretly against Nazis
L - 7. HIRSH	G.	Pretend dead aunt
T - 8. BODYGUARD	H.	Fatihful dog of Mama's
Y - 9. FIREWORKS	I.	Delivered by Annemarie to Henrik
I - 10. HANDKERCHIEF	J.	Coast of Denmark near Sweden
H - 11. TROFAST	K.	Used to prevent Ellen's detection
K - 12. PHOTOGRAPH	L.	Button shop lady, Mrs. _____
D - 13. DANSKE	M.	Trick to fool Nazis
V - 14. OCCUPATION	N.	Nazi symbol
U - 15. HOLOCAUST	O.	Danish money
X - 16. CUPCAKES	P.	Cause of Great Aunt Birte's death
C - 17. BALTIC	Q.	Borders Denmark to the west, _____ Sea
F - 18. RESISTANCE	R.	How Mama looked when she broke her ankle
G - 19. BIRTE	S.	Kirsti's kitten; God of _____
P - 20. TYPHUS	T.	All of Denmark is King Christian's
E - 21. TRUNK	U.	Persecution of Jews by Nazis
B - 22. PSALM	V.	Nazi soldiers patrolling in Denmark, Nazi _____
Q - 23. NORTH	W.	Copenhagen fun spot, Tivoli _____
J - 24. GILLELEJE	X.	Pink frosted ones were nowhere to be found
S - 25. THUNDER	Y.	Explosion of Danish naval fleet on Kirsti's bday

Number the Stars Matching 2

___ 1. TRUNK   A. Author
___ 2. BLOSSOM   B. Contains words in title of book
___ 3. OSTERBROGADE   C. Setting
___ 4. CROCHETING   D. Smuggled Jews out of Denmark
___ 5. SWASTIKA   E. Worked secretly against Nazis
___ 6. BIRTE   F. Lise's trousseau is in it
___ 7. INGEBORG   G. Mrs. Johansen did this the night Lise was killed
___ 8. LOWRY   H. Copenhagen street
___ 9. LISE   I. North Sea channel between Sweden and Denmark
___10. SPECIAL   J. Pretend dead aunt
___11. AMALIENBORG   K. Once you're greeted by a king
___12. GILLELEJE   L. Borders Denmark to the east, _____ Sea
___13. ELLEN   M. Obstinate younger sister of Annemarie
___14. DENMARK   N. Older sister of Annemarie and Kirsti
___15. KATTEGAT   O. Provided family with milk
___16. COFFIN   P. Strong Jewish trait
___17. ROSEN   Q. Jewish friend of Annemarie
___18. PRIDE   R. Capital of Denmark
___19. HANDKERCHIEF   S. Coast of Denmark near Sweden
___20. BALTIC   T. Delivered by Annemarie to Henrik
___21. HENRIK   U. Hid blankets and clothes
___22. RESISTANCE   V. Fisherman who lives by the sea, Uncle _____
___23. KIRSTI   W. Copenhagen palace
___24. PSALM   X. Jewish schoolteacher, Mr. _____
___25. COPENHAGEN   Y. Nazi symbol

Number the Stars Matching 2 Answer Key

F - 1.	TRUNK	A.	Author
O - 2.	BLOSSOM	B.	Contains words in title of book
H - 3.	OSTERBROGADE	C.	Setting
G - 4.	CROCHETING	D.	Smuggled Jews out of Denmark
Y - 5.	SWASTIKA	E.	Worked secretly against Nazis
J - 6.	BIRTE	F.	Lise's trousseau is in it
D - 7.	INGEBORG	G.	Mrs. Johansen did this the night Lise was killed
A - 8.	LOWRY	H.	Copenhagen street
N - 9.	LISE	I.	North Sea channel between Sweden and Denmark
K - 10.	SPECIAL	J.	Pretend dead aunt
W - 11.	AMALIENBORG	K.	Once you're greeted by a king
S - 12.	GILLELEJE	L.	Borders Denmark to the east, _____ Sea
Q - 13.	ELLEN	M.	Obstinate younger sister of Annemarie
C - 14.	DENMARK	N.	Older sister of Annemarie and Kirsti
I - 15.	KATTEGAT	O.	Provided family with milk
U - 16.	COFFIN	P.	Strong Jewish trait
X - 17.	ROSEN	Q.	Jewish friend of Annemarie
P - 18.	PRIDE	R.	Capital of Denmark
T - 19.	HANDKERCHIEF	S.	Coast of Denmark near Sweden
L - 20.	BALTIC	T.	Delivered by Annemarie to Henrik
V - 21.	HENRIK	U.	Hid blankets and clothes
E - 22.	RESISTANCE	V.	Fisherman who lives by the sea, Uncle _____
M - 23.	KIRSTI	W.	Copenhagen palace
B - 24.	PSALM	X.	Jewish schoolteacher, Mr. _____
R - 25.	COPENHAGEN	Y.	Nazi symbol

Number the Stars Matching 3

___ 1. LOWRY   A. Cause of Great Aunt Birte's death
___ 2. TROFAST   B. All of Denmark is King Christian's
___ 3. CHRISTIAN   C. Obstinate younger sister of Annemarie
___ 4. KIRSTI   D. None is available during war
___ 5. PHOTOGRAPH   E. Older sister of Annemarie and Kirsti
___ 6. TYPHUS   F. Pretend dead aunt
___ 7. TRUNK   G. King Christian's faithful horse
___ 8. BODYGUARD   H. Jewish schoolteacher, Mr. _____
___ 9. ANNEMARIE   I. Fisherman who lives by the sea, Uncle _____
___ 10. SLAPPED   J. Used to prevent Ellen's detection
___ 11. LEATHER   K. Courageous young Danish girl
___ 12. PETER   L. Provided family with milk
___ 13. INGEBORG   M. Kirsti's kitten; God of _____
___ 14. HENRIK   N. Nazi soldier did this to Mama
___ 15. ROSEN   O. Jewish friend of Annemarie
___ 16. OSTERBROGADE   P. Copenhagen street
___ 17. BIRTE   Q. Fatiful dog of Mama's
___ 18. JUBILEE   R. Trick to fool Nazis
___ 19. PRIDE   S. Smuggled Jews out of Denmark
___ 20. THUNDER   T. Lise's trousseau is in it
___ 21. ELLEN   U. Author
___ 22. FUNERAL   V. Danish king, _____ the tenth
___ 23. LISE   W. Red-headed fiance of Lise
___ 24. CROCHETING   X. Strong Jewish trait
___ 25. BLOSSOM   Y. Mrs. Johansen did this the night Lise was killed

Number the Stars Matching 3 Answer Key

U - 1. LOWRY	A. Cause of Great Aunt Birte's death
Q - 2. TROFAST	B. All of Denmark is King Christian's
V - 3. CHRISTIAN	C. Obstinate younger sister of Annemarie
C - 4. KIRSTI	D. None is available during war
J - 5. PHOTOGRAPH	E. Older sister of Annemarie and Kirsti
A - 6. TYPHUS	F. Pretend dead aunt
T - 7. TRUNK	G. King Christian's faithful horse
B - 8. BODYGUARD	H. Jewish schoolteacher, Mr. _____
K - 9. ANNEMARIE	I. Fisherman who lives by the sea, Uncle _____
N -10. SLAPPED	J. Used to prevent Ellen's detection
D -11. LEATHER	K. Courageous young Danish girl
W -12. PETER	L. Provided family with milk
S -13. INGEBORG	M. Kirsti's kitten; God of _____
I - 14. HENRIK	N. Nazi soldier did this to Mama
H -15. ROSEN	O. Jewish friend of Annemarie
P -16. OSTERBROGADE	P. Copenhagen street
F -17. BIRTE	Q. Fatihful dog of Mama's
G -18. JUBILEE	R. Trick to fool Nazis
X -19. PRIDE	S. Smuggled Jews out of Denmark
M -20. THUNDER	T. Lise's trousseau is in it
O -21. ELLEN	U. Author
R -22. FUNERAL	V. Danish king, _____ the tenth
E -23. LISE	W. Red-headed fiance of Lise
Y -24. CROCHETING	X. Strong Jewish trait
L -25. BLOSSOM	Y. Mrs. Johansen did this the night Lise was killed

Number the Stars Matching 4

___ 1. LEATHER   A. King Christian's faithful horse
___ 2. GONE   B. Older sister of Annemarie and Kirsti
___ 3. JUBILEE   C. Author
___ 4. FISH SHOES   D. Pink frosted ones were nowhere to be found
___ 5. SWEDEN   E. Copenhagen fun spot, Tivoli _____
___ 6. HOLOCAUST   F. Smuggled Jews out of Denmark
___ 7. HANDKERCHIEF   G. North Sea channel between Sweden and Denmark
___ 8. TROFAST   H. Jews were taken to this place by boat
___ 9. LOWRY   I. Fatihful dog of Mama's
___10. CHRISTIAN   J. Capital of Denmark
___11. AMALIENBORG   K. Delivered by Annemarie to Henrik
___12. NORTH   L. None is available during war
___13. CROCHETING   M. Borders Denmark to the east, _____ Sea
___14. LISE   N. Mrs. Johansen did this the night Lise was killed
___15. KATTEGAT   O. Provided family with milk
___16. GARDENS   P. Lise's trousseau is in it
___17. BLOSSOM   Q. Kirsti refused to wear
___18. PETER   R. Button shop lady, Mrs. _____
___19. COPENHAGEN   S. Danish king, _____ the tenth
___20. TRUNK   T. Copenhagen palace
___21. BALTIC   U. Red-headed fiance of Lise
___22. CUPCAKES   V. Mama's favorite story, _____ With The Wind
___23. INGEBORG   W. Borders Denmark to the west, _____ Sea
___24. HIRSH   X. Explosion of Danish naval fleet on Kirsti's bday
___25. FIREWORKS   Y. Persecution of Jews by Nazis

Number the Stars Matching 4 Answer Key

L - 1.	LEATHER	A.	King Christian's faithful horse
V - 2.	GONE	B.	Older sister of Annemarie and Kirsti
A - 3.	JUBILEE	C.	Author
Q - 4.	FISH SHOES	D.	Pink frosted ones were nowhere to be found
H - 5.	SWEDEN	E.	Copenhagen fun spot, Tivoli _____
Y - 6.	HOLOCAUST	F.	Smuggled Jews out of Denmark
K - 7.	HANDKERCHIEF	G.	North Sea channel between Sweden and Denmark
I - 8.	TROFAST	H.	Jews were taken to this place by boat
C - 9.	LOWRY	I.	Fatihful dog of Mama's
S -10.	CHRISTIAN	J.	Capital of Denmark
T -11.	AMALIENBORG	K.	Delivered by Annemarie to Henrik
W -12.	NORTH	L.	None is available during war
N -13.	CROCHETING	M.	Borders Denmark to the east, _____ Sea
B -14.	LISE	N.	Mrs. Johansen did this the night Lise was killed
G -15.	KATTEGAT	O.	Provided family with milk
E -16.	GARDENS	P.	Lise's trousseau is in it
O -17.	BLOSSOM	Q.	Kirsti refused to wear
U -18.	PETER	R.	Button shop lady, Mrs. _____
J -19.	COPENHAGEN	S.	Danish king, _____ the tenth
P -20.	TRUNK	T.	Copenhagen palace
M -21.	BALTIC	U.	Red-headed fiance of Lise
D -22.	CUPCAKES	V.	Mama's favorite story, _____ With The Wind
F -23.	INGEBORG	W.	Borders Denmark to the west, _____ Sea
R -24.	HIRSH	X.	Explosion of Danish naval fleet on Kirsti's bday
X -25.	FIREWORKS	Y.	Persecution of Jews by Nazis

Number the Stars Magic Squares 1

Match the definition with the vocabulary word. Put your answers in the magic squares below. When your answers are correct, all columns and rows will add to the same number.

A. SPECIAL
B. RESISTANCE
C. BLOSSOM
D. BALTIC
E. BIRTE
F. RUCKSACK
G. HIRSH
H. PRIDE
I. SWEDEN
J. GIRAFFE
K. SEASICK
L. AMALIENBORG
M. LISE
N. CUPCAKES
O. COFFIN
P. GARDENS

1. Pink frosted ones were nowhere to be found
2. Button shop lady, Mrs. _____
3. Copenhagen palace
4. Once you're greeted by a king
5. How Mrs. Rosen felt in the boat
6. Worked secretly against Nazis
7. Older sister of Annemarie and Kirsti
8. Strong Jewish trait
9. Pretend dead aunt
10. Copenhagen fun spot, Tivoli _____
11. Provided family with milk
12. Nickname for tall Nazi soldier
13. Borders Denmark to the east, _____ Sea
14. Jews were taken to this place by boat
15. Girls' bookbag
16. Hid blankets and clothes

A=	B=	C=	D=
E=	F=	G=	H=
I=	J=	K=	L=
M=	N=	O=	P=

Number the Stars Magic Squares 1 Answer Key

Match the definition with the vocabulary word. Put your answers in the magic squares below. When your answers are correct, all columns and rows will add to the same number.

A. SPECIAL
B. RESISTANCE
C. BLOSSOM
D. BALTIC
E. BIRTE
F. RUCKSACK
G. HIRSH
H. PRIDE
I. SWEDEN
J. GIRAFFE
K. SEASICK
L. AMALIENBORG
M. LISE
N. CUPCAKES
O. COFFIN
P. GARDENS

1. Pink frosted ones were nowhere to be found
2. Button shop lady, Mrs. _____
3. Copenhagen palace
4. Once you're greeted by a king
5. How Mrs. Rosen felt in the boat
6. Worked secretly against Nazis
7. Older sister of Annemarie and Kirsti
8. Strong Jewish trait
9. Pretend dead aunt
10. Copenhagen fun spot, Tivoli _____
11. Provided family with milk
12. Nickname for tall Nazi soldier
13. Borders Denmark to the east, _____ Sea
14. Jews were taken to this place by boat
15. Girls' bookbag
16. Hid blankets and clothes

A=4	B=6	C=11	D=13
E=9	F=15	G=2	H=8
I=14	J=12	K=5	L=3
M=7	N=1	O=16	P=10

Number the Stars Magic Squares 2

Match the definition with the vocabulary word. Put your answers in the magic squares below. When your answers are correct, all columns and rows will add to the same number.

A. BLOSSOM
B. SPECIAL
C. BODYGUARD
D. FIREWORKS
E. LISE
F. KIRSTI
G. HENRIK
H. HANDKERCHIEF
I. ELLEN
J. LEATHER
K. LOWRY
L. BIRTE
M. STAR
N. AMALIENBORG
O. GARDENS
P. SWEDEN

1. Symbol of Jewish faith, _____ of David
2. Obstinate younger sister of Annemarie
3. Delivered by Annemarie to Henrik
4. Copenhagen fun spot, Tivoli _____
5. Pretend dead aunt
6. All of Denmark is King Christian's
7. Provided family with milk
8. None is available during war
9. Author
10. Explosion of Danish naval fleet on Kirsti's bday
11. Once you're greeted by a king
12. Jewish friend of Annemarie
13. Copenhagen palace
14. Older sister of Annemarie and Kirsti
15. Fisherman who lives by the sea, Uncle _____
16. Jews were taken to this place by boat

A=	B=	C=	D=
E=	F=	G=	H=
I=	J=	K=	L=
M=	N=	O=	P=

Number the Stars Magic Squares 2 Answer Key

Match the definition with the vocabulary word. Put your answers in the magic squares below. When your answers are correct, all columns and rows will add to the same number.

A. BLOSSOM
B. SPECIAL
C. BODYGUARD
D. FIREWORKS
E. LISE
F. KIRSTI
G. HENRIK
H. HANDKERCHIEF
I. ELLEN
J. LEATHER
K. LOWRY
L. BIRTE
M. STAR
N. AMALIENBORG
O. GARDENS
P. SWEDEN

1. Symbol of Jewish faith, _____ of David
2. Obstinate younger sister of Annemarie
3. Delivered by Annemarie to Henrik
4. Copenhagen fun spot, Tivoli _____
5. Pretend dead aunt
6. All of Denmark is King Christian's
7. Provided family with milk
8. None is available during war
9. Author
10. Explosion of Danish naval fleet on Kirsti's bday
11. Once you're greeted by a king
12. Jewish friend of Annemarie
13. Copenhagen palace
14. Older sister of Annemarie and Kirsti
15. Fisherman who lives by the sea, Uncle _____
16. Jews were taken to this place by boat

A=7	B=11	C=6	D=10
E=14	F=2	G=15	H=3
I=12	J=8	K=9	L=5
M=1	N=13	O=4	P=16

Number the Stars Magic Squares 3

Match the definition with the vocabulary word. Put your answers in the magic squares below. When your answers are correct, all columns and rows will add to the same number.

A. SPECIAL
B. ANDERSON
C. PRIDE
D. TRUNK
E. DRUNKARD
F. COFFIN
G. BODYGUARD
H. KATTEGAT
I. THUNDER
J. KRONER
K. DANSKE
L. SWASTIKA
M. HIRSH
N. DENMARK
O. ROSEN
P. BLOSSOM

1. Once you're greeted by a king
2. Setting
3. Danish money
4. How Mama looked when she broke her ankle
5. All of Denmark is King Christian's
6. Nazi symbol
7. Provided family with milk
8. Strong Jewish trait
9. Jewish schoolteacher, Mr. _____
10. Lise's trousseau is in it
11. North Sea channel between Sweden and Denmark
12. De Frie _____
13. Kirsti's kitten; God of _____
14. Hid blankets and clothes
15. Danish fairy tale author, Hans Christian _____
16. Button shop lady, Mrs. _____

A=	B=	C=	D=
E=	F=	G=	H=
I=	J=	K=	L=
M=	N=	O=	P=

Number the Stars Magic Squares 3 Answer Key

Match the definition with the vocabulary word. Put your answers in the magic squares below. When your answers are correct, all columns and rows will add to the same number.

A. SPECIAL
B. ANDERSON
C. PRIDE
D. TRUNK
E. DRUNKARD
F. COFFIN
G. BODYGUARD
H. KATTEGAT
I. THUNDER
J. KRONER
K. DANSKE
L. SWASTIKA
M. HIRSH
N. DENMARK
O. ROSEN
P. BLOSSOM

1. Once you're greeted by a king
2. Setting
3. Danish money
4. How Mama looked when she broke her ankle
5. All of Denmark is King Christian's
6. Nazi symbol
7. Provided family with milk
8. Strong Jewish trait
9. Jewish schoolteacher, Mr. _____
10. Lise's trousseau is in it
11. North Sea channel between Sweden and Denmark
12. De Frie _____
13. Kirsti's kitten; God of _____
14. Hid blankets and clothes
15. Danish fairy tale author, Hans Christian _____
16. Button shop lady, Mrs. _____

A=1	B=15	C=8	D=10
E=4	F=14	G=5	H=11
I=13	J=3	K=12	L=6
M=16	N=2	O=9	P=7

Number the Stars Magic Squares 4

Match the definition with the vocabulary word. Put your answers in the magic squares below. When your answers are correct, all columns and rows will add to the same number.

A. BIRTE
B. ROSEN
C. TRUNK
D. THUNDER
E. LOWRY
F. COPENHAGEN
G. LEATHER
H. SWASTIKA
I. ELLEN
J. PRIDE
K. HENRIK
L. TYPHUS
M. BALTIC
N. SLAPPED
O. FUNERAL
P. PETER

1. Lise's trousseau is in it
2. Strong Jewish trait
3. Capital of Denmark
4. Trick to fool Nazis
5. Red-headed fiance of Lise
6. Author
7. Jewish friend of Annemarie
8. Kirsti's kitten; God of _____
9. Borders Denmark to the east, _____ Sea
10. Nazi symbol
11. Cause of Great Aunt Birte's death
12. Pretend dead aunt
13. Jewish schoolteacher, Mr. _____
14. Fisherman who lives by the sea, Uncle _____
15. None is available during war
16. Nazi soldier did this to Mama

A=	B=	C=	D=
E=	F=	G=	H=
I=	J=	K=	L=
M=	N=	O=	P=

Number the Stars Magic Squares 4 Answer Key

Match the definition with the vocabulary word. Put your answers in the magic squares below. When your answers are correct, all columns and rows will add to the same number.

A. BIRTE
B. ROSEN
C. TRUNK
D. THUNDER
E. LOWRY
F. COPENHAGEN
G. LEATHER
H. SWASTIKA
I. ELLEN
J. PRIDE
K. HENRIK
L. TYPHUS
M. BALTIC
N. SLAPPED
O. FUNERAL
P. PETER

1. Lise's trousseau is in it
2. Strong Jewish trait
3. Capital of Denmark
4. Trick to fool Nazis
5. Red-headed fiance of Lise
6. Author
7. Jewish friend of Annemarie
8. Kirsti's kitten; God of _____
9. Borders Denmark to the east, _____ Sea
10. Nazi symbol
11. Cause of Great Aunt Birte's death
12. Pretend dead aunt
13. Jewish schoolteacher, Mr. _____
14. Fisherman who lives by the sea, Uncle _____
15. None is available during war
16. Nazi soldier did this to Mama

A=12	B=13	C=1	D=8
E=6	F=3	G=15	H=10
I=7	J=2	K=14	L=11
M=9	N=16	O=4	P=5

Number the Stars Word Search 1

```
R P W F Z T R O F A S T P S A L M Q
D U Z C E Z V I E B K C I S A E S H
X R C T I T S R I K O E B R T Z H X
H Y R K P H G V H B D D E L L E N K
Q I N C S A S R C I A N Y R W O L R
B L M H R A K P R N U L Z G T C E A
L Y O D E H C P E F X J T V U D C M
O E E E N J H K K C N G X I N A H N
S N J F O V F E D F I S D U C G R E
S O K F R E K S N A D A H T R O N D
O S K A K Y R A A R T T L P K I R F
M R B R T V I X H G I S B E F E N R
R E S I S T A N C E W K E F S E E W
P D H G S Y E W L E B L O S S H S K
Z N I I B P C G D F I C G I T R O G
X A R T N H F E A B G S L A A M R M
D H S T R U N K U T R P E T E R C T
C J H D Z S S J V B N L S G O N E K
```

All of Denmark is King Christian's (9)
Author (5)
Borders Denmark to the east, _____ Sea (6)
Borders Denmark to the west, _____ Sea (5)
Button shop lady, Mrs. _____ (5)
Cause of Great Aunt Birte's death (6)
Contains words in title of book (5)
Copenhagen fun spot, Tivoli _____ (7)
Danish fairy tale author, Hans Christian _____ (8)
Danish king, _____ the tenth (9)
Danish money (6)
De Frie _____ (6)
Delivered by Annemarie to Henrik (12)
Fatihful dog of Mama's (7)
Fisherman who lives by the sea, Uncle _____ (6)
Girls' bookbag (8)
Hid blankets and clothes (6)
How Mrs. Rosen felt in the boat (7)
Jewish friend of Annemarie (5)
Jewish schoolteacher, Mr. _____ (5)
Jews were taken to this place by boat (6)

King Christian's faithful horse (7)
Kirsti refused to wear (10)
Kirsti's kitten; God of _____ (7)
Lise danced in it on her engagement, yellow _____ (5)
Lise's trousseau is in it (5)
Mama's favorite story, _____ With The Wind (4)
Nickname for tall Nazi soldier (7)
None is available during war (7)
North Sea channel between Sweden and Denmark (8)
Obstinate younger sister of Annemarie (6)
Older sister of Annemarie and Kirsti (4)
Once you're greeted by a king (7)
Pretend dead aunt (5)
Provided family with milk (7)
Red-headed fiance of Lise (5)
Setting (7)
Strong Jewish trait (5)
Symbol of Jewish faith, _____ of David (4)
Trick to fool Nazis (7)
Worked secretly against Nazis (10)

Number the Stars Word Search 1 Answer Key

```
R           T  R  O  F  A  S  T  P  S  A  L  M
   U     E        I  E  B  K  C  I  S  A  E  S
      C  T  I  T  S  R  I  K  O  E     R
      R  K     H  G     H  B  D  D  E  L  L  E  N  K
   I        S  A  S     C  I  A  N  Y  R  W  O  L  R
B        H  R  A     P  R     U  L     G        E  A
L     O  D  E     C  P  E  F        T     U  D     M
O  E  E  E  N     H  K  K  C              I  N  A  N
S  N     F  O           E  D        I     U  C     R  E
S  O  K  F  R  E  K  S  N  A  D  A  H  T  R  O  N  D
O  S     A  K        A  A  R     T  L        I  R
M  R     R  T     I     H     I  S     E  F  E  N  R
R  E  S  I  S  T  A  N  C  E  W  K  E  F  S  E  E
   D  H  G  S  Y  E        E        L  O  S  S  H  S
   N  I  I     P     G  D        I  C     I  T  R  O
   A  R        H     E  A  B        L  A  A     R
   H  S  T  R  U  N  K  U  T        P  E  T  E  R
C     H        S        J           L  S  G  O  N  E
```

All of Denmark is King Christian's (9)
Author (5)
Borders Denmark to the east,
_____ Sea (6)
Borders Denmark to the west,
_____ Sea (5)
Button shop lady, Mrs. _____ (5)
Cause of Great Aunt Birte's death (6)
Contains words in title of book (5)
Copenhagen fun spot, Tivoli
_____ (7)
Danish fairy tale author, Hans Christian
_____ (8)
Danish king, _____ the
tenth (9)
Danish money (6)
De Frie _____ (6)
Delivered by Annemarie to Henrik (12)
Fatihful dog of Mama's (7)
Fisherman who lives by the sea, Uncle
_____ (6)
Girls' bookbag (8)
Hid blankets and clothes (6)
How Mrs. Rosen felt in the boat (7)
Jewish friend of Annemarie (5)
Jewish schoolteacher, Mr. _____
(5)
Jews were taken to this place by boat (6)

King Christian's faithful horse (7)
Kirsti refused to wear (10)
Kirsti's kitten; God of _____ (7)
Lise danced in it on her engagement, yellow
_____ (5)
Lise's trousseau is in it (5)
Mama's favorite story, _____ With
The Wind (4)
Nickname for tall Nazi soldier (7)
None is available during war (7)
North Sea channel between Sweden and
Denmark (8)
Obstinate younger sister of Annemarie (6)
Older sister of Annemarie and Kirsti (4)
Once you're greeted by a king (7)
Pretend dead aunt (5)
Provided family with milk (7)
Red-headed fiance of Lise (5)
Setting (7)
Strong Jewish trait (5)
Symbol of Jewish faith, _____ of David
(4)
Trick to fool Nazis (7)
Worked secretly against Nazis (10)

Number the Stars Word Search 2

```
F J K C A S K C U R H G Y D H N N R
E I R A M E N N A N L Z O P W O E H
L J A M M O T D T P T B B N E R L L
H G M Z S H H R R M P R L L E T L M
A M N R U S I B U P R A E O E H E H
O N E N S H R F N A I T A W S V H R
P S D R E S S R K C D Y T R I S D W
C E T E T I H I E S E P H Y L R O J
R K D E R F T P P S L H E E A M G M
O A I N R S S R S Q I U R K N F S I
C C T N A B O S A G N S N B I R T E
H P F W G N R N L C I U T R S S I E
E U S C D E Z O M A R R E A R T E K
T C W O A S B M G D P W A I N L A N
I C E F N O C O L A O P K F I C Y R
N B D F S R K J R R D V E B F T E Y
G F E I K L D Q K G V E U D P E Q W
Q S N N E J D S X J K J K R O N E R
```

Author (5)
Borders Denmark to the west, _____ Sea (5)
Button shop lady, Mrs. _____ (5)
Cause of Great Aunt Birte's death (6)
Contains words in title of book (5)
Copenhagen street (12)
Courageous young Danish girl (9)
Danish fairy tale author, Hans Christian _____ (8)
Danish money (6)
De Frie _____ (6)
Explosion of Danish naval fleet on Kirsti's bday (9)
Fisherman who lives by the sea, Uncle _____ (6)
Girls' bookbag (8)
Hid blankets and clothes (6)
How Mama looked when she broke her ankle (8)
Jewish friend of Annemarie (5)
Jewish schoolteacher, Mr. _____ (5)
Jews were taken to this place by boat (6)
King Christian's faithful horse (7)
Kirsti refused to wear (10)
Kirsti's kitten; God of _____ (7)
Lise danced in it on her engagement, yellow

_____ (5)
Lise's trousseau is in it (5)
Mama's favorite story, _____ With The Wind (4)
Mrs. Johansen did this the night Lise was killed (10)
Nazi soldier did this to Mama (7)
Nazi symbol (8)
Nickname for tall Nazi soldier (7)
None is available during war (7)
Obstinate younger sister of Annemarie (6)
Older sister of Annemarie and Kirsti (4)
Once you're greeted by a king (7)
Pink frosted ones were nowhere to be found (8)
Pretend dead aunt (5)
Provided family with milk (7)
Red-headed fiance of Lise (5)
Setting (7)
Smuggled Jews out of Denmark (8)
Strong Jewish trait (5)
Symbol of Jewish faith, _____ of David (4)
Worked secretly against Nazis (10)

Number the Stars Word Search 2 Answer Key

Author (5)
Borders Denmark to the west, _____ Sea (5)
Button shop lady, Mrs. _____ (5)
Cause of Great Aunt Birte's death (6)
Contains words in title of book (5)
Copenhagen street (12)
Courageous young Danish girl (9)
Danish fairy tale author, Hans Christian _____ (8)
Danish money (6)
De Frie _____ (6)
Explosion of Danish naval fleet on Kirsti's bday (9)
Fisherman who lives by the sea, Uncle _____ (6)
Girls' bookbag (8)
Hid blankets and clothes (6)
How Mama looked when she broke her ankle (8)
Jewish friend of Annemarie (5)
Jewish schoolteacher, Mr. _____ (5)
Jews were taken to this place by boat (6)
King Christian's faithful horse (7)
Kirsti refused to wear (10)
Kirsti's kitten; God of _____ (7)
Lise danced in it on her engagement, yellow _____ (5)
Lise's trousseau is in it (5)
Mama's favorite story, _____ With The Wind (4)
Mrs. Johansen did this the night Lise was killed (10)
Nazi soldier did this to Mama (7)
Nazi symbol (8)
Nickname for tall Nazi soldier (7)
None is available during war (7)
Obstinate younger sister of Annemarie (6)
Older sister of Annemarie and Kirsti (4)
Once you're greeted by a king (7)
Pink frosted ones were nowhere to be found (8)
Pretend dead aunt (5)
Provided family with milk (7)
Red-headed fiance of Lise (5)
Setting (7)
Smuggled Jews out of Denmark (8)
Strong Jewish trait (5)
Symbol of Jewish faith, _____ of David (4)
Worked secretly against Nazis (10)

Number the Stars Word Search 3

```
P H O T O G R A P H S I L P F T F X K R
N A S C R X C R T N Q N B R W R I V A P
D N R Z M U X M E N N G A I H O S B T F
G D E X F S N D K A V E N D V F H Q T C
N K S D V N R K I B P B D E J A S N E K
I E I D O A M T R F W O E P N S H L G B
T R S R G Z S Y S L N R R T G T O I A B
E C T F S I R J T O B G S X X Q E S T M
H H A M R W Y F I R E W O R K S S E O P
C I N H O S E T Q T P G N G S T J S Q P
O E C L H D A D M H J E O G A E S C Y H
R F E Y R P E C E U S N T R L O G C F T
C O Z E U E K I R N E H E E L I B U J Q
O J S C J L S T M D A O L B R X N P L N
F S C E W L N L F E S L S L D E H C T F
F O W L N E A A R R I O P E R M I A X M
I B D A B N D B T G C C F A Q Q R K Q V
N R E I S O R C Y W K A L T T F S E B D
W F N C V T D U Q R W U N H H Y H S R F
X R M E N N I Y C T K S K E N K P A X J
S L A P P E D K G K G T M R F B K H E Q
D V R S T Y X G A U S L T C O N T T U M
D H K T N L B X X N A A Y P U N R Y T S
A N N E M A R I E S H R C R S I E N R X
G I R A F F E N P F B K D K B C Y R S B
```

ANDERSON	ELLEN	KATTEGAT	RUCKSACK
ANNEMARIE	FIREWORKS	KIRSTI	SEASICK
BALTIC	FISH SHOES	KRONER	SLAPPED
BIRTE	FUNERAL	LEATHER	SPECIAL
BLOSSOM	GARDENS	LISE	STAR
BODYGUARD	GILLELEJE	LOWRY	SWASTIKA
CHRISTIAN	GIRAFFE	NORTH	SWEDEN
COFFIN	GONE	OCCUPATION	THUNDER
CROCHETING	HANDKERCHIEF	PETER	TROFAST
CUPCAKES	HENRIK	PHOTOGRAPH	TRUNK
DANSKE	HIRSH	PRIDE	TYPHUS
DENMARK	HOLOCAUST	PSALM	
DRESS	INGEBORG	RESISTANCE	
DRUNKARD	JUBILEE	ROSEN	

Number the Stars Word Search 3 Answer Key

ANDERSON	ELLEN	KATTEGAT	RUCKSACK
ANNEMARIE	FIREWORKS	KIRSTI	SEASICK
BALTIC	FISH SHOES	KRONER	SLAPPED
BIRTE	FUNERAL	LEATHER	SPECIAL
BLOSSOM	GARDENS	LISE	STAR
BODYGUARD	GILLELEJE	LOWRY	SWASTIKA
CHRISTIAN	GIRAFFE	NORTH	SWEDEN
COFFIN	GONE	OCCUPATION	THUNDER
CROCHETING	HANDKERCHIEF	PETER	TROFAST
CUPCAKES	HENRIK	PHOTOGRAPH	TRUNK
DANSKE	HIRSH	PRIDE	TYPHUS
DENMARK	HOLOCAUST	PSALM	
DRESS	INGEBORG	RESISTANCE	
DRUNKARD	JUBILEE	ROSEN	

Number the Stars Word Search 4

```
C O F F I N C O P E N H A G E N J A J G
H S T F I I L B V K L M L I R J D N R J
R T S P T S Z F R S A X V L Q Y V D V V
I E U L H C H A R L Y D L L M J R E F T
S R A R B O M S I G N I T E H C O R C W
T B C R E N T E H T G D H L A P R S W J
I R O Y E S N O A O R K U E W T R O M T
A O L D K B I G G A E P N J D B H N T A
N G O P O S E S U R I S D E M A D E N G
K A H R F T L G T T A H E Y J B N N R J
K D G G T F Y A S A W P R V C J E S D P
W E G A R D G R P C N W H U H M H M K K
S S K X O Y I I F P D C P L A D X B C E
O W T B F K N S R F E C E R N M R I E Y
C R A D A T R I O A A D I D D J S B S B
C X T S S E D Q S K F E Y H K A Z N I C
U B I R T E E L L E N U F S P E C I A L S
P Y D E A I R S N D N I E S R N L X S S
A R P K R S K Y R G E R E U C G R E S H
T G O N E V W A R A R E L H H S R I H B
I M G U Y H K E D R A W I P I D C W K M
O Z S R Z N N R D D L O B Y E R X K L Z
N X W T U O V M P E R R U T F G M A J F
R O P R R C M X M N K J B L O S S O M
L B D K N O R T H S B S P J M P F Q Q B
```

AMALIENBORG	DRESS	JUBILEE	RESISTANCE
ANDERSON	DRUNKARD	KATTEGAT	ROSEN
ANNEMARIE	ELLEN	KIRSTI	SEASICK
BALTIC	FIREWORKS	KRONER	SLAPPED
BIRTE	FISH SHOES	LEATHER	SPECIAL
BLOSSOM	FUNERAL	LISE	STAR
BODYGUARD	GARDENS	LOWRY	SWASTIKA
CHRISTIAN	GILLELEJE	NORTH	SWEDEN
COFFIN	GIRAFFE	OCCUPATION	THUNDER
COPENHAGEN	GONE	OSTERBROGADE	TROFAST
CROCHETING	HANDKERCHIEF	PETER	TRUNK
CUPCAKES	HENRIK	PHOTOGRAPH	TYPHUS
DANSKE	HIRSH	PRIDE	
DENMARK	HOLOCAUST	PSALM	

Number the Stars Word Search 4 Answer Key

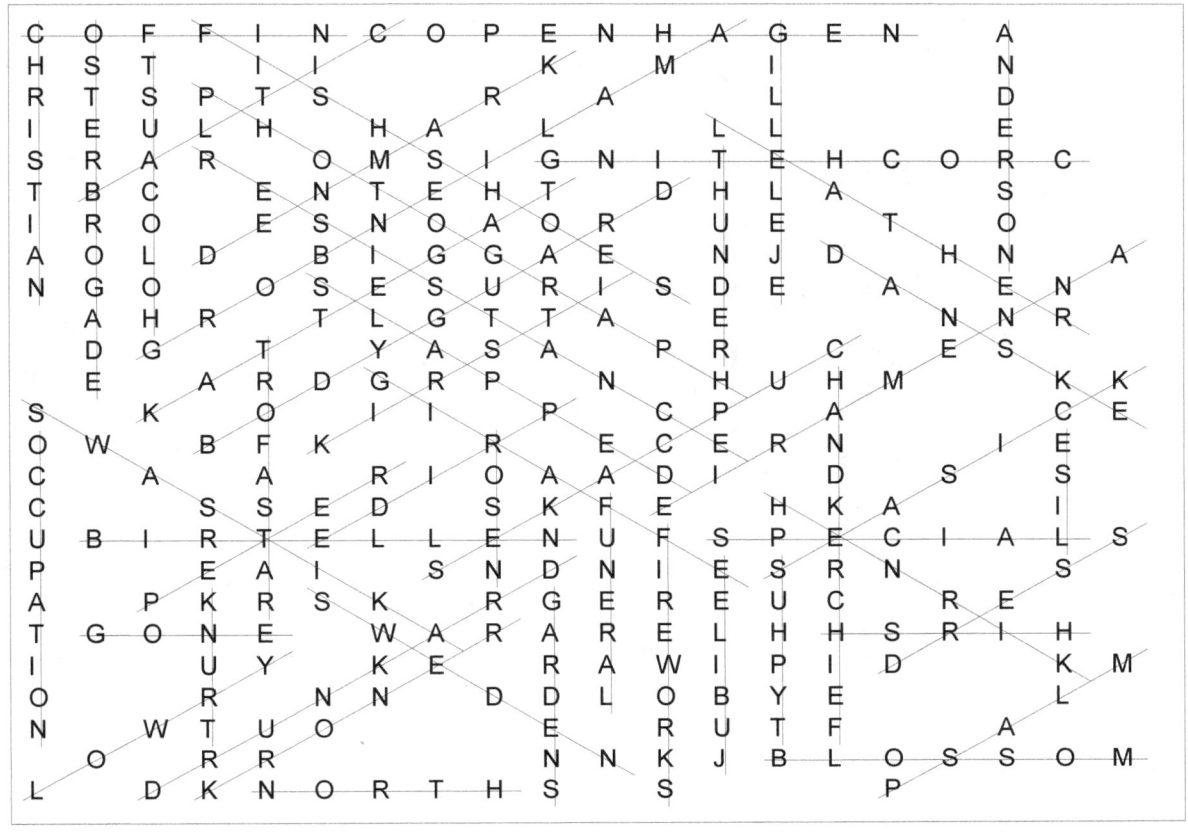

AMALIENBORG	DRESS	JUBILEE	RESISTANCE
ANDERSON	DRUNKARD	KATTEGAT	ROSEN
ANNEMARIE	ELLEN	KIRSTI	SEASICK
BALTIC	FIREWORKS	KRONER	SLAPPED
BIRTE	FISH SHOES	LEATHER	SPECIAL
BLOSSOM	FUNERAL	LISE	STAR
BODYGUARD	GARDENS	LOWRY	SWASTIKA
CHRISTIAN	GILLELEJE	NORTH	SWEDEN
COFFIN	GIRAFFE	OCCUPATION	THUNDER
COPENHAGEN	GONE	OSTERBROGADE	TROFAST
CROCHETING	HANDKERCHIEF	PETER	TRUNK
CUPCAKES	HENRIK	PHOTOGRAPH	TYPHUS
DANSKE	HIRSH	PRIDE	
DENMARK	HOLOCAUST	PSALM	

Number the Stars Crossword 1

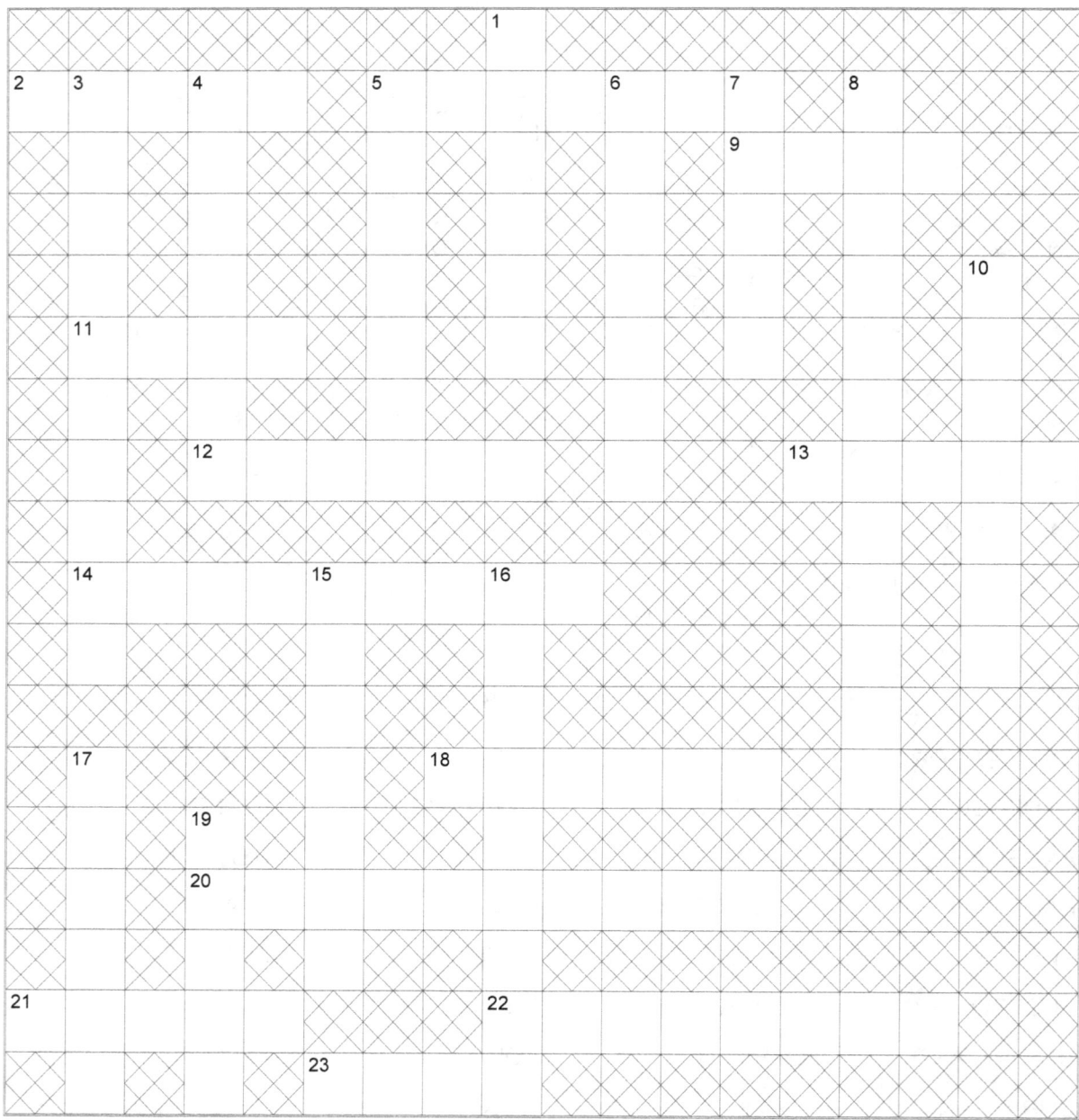

Across
2. Strong Jewish trait
5. Nickname for tall Nazi soldier
9. Older sister of Annemarie and Kirsti
11. Symbol of Jewish faith, _____ of David
12. Obstinate younger sister of Annemarie
13. Lise's trousseau is in it
14. Danish king, _____ the tenth
18. Fisherman who lives by the sea, Uncle_____
20. Nazi soldiers patrolling in Denmark, Nazi _____
21. Pretend dead aunt
22. Smuggled Jews out of Denmark
23. Mama's favorite story, _____ With The Wind

Down
1. Danish money
3. Worked secretly against Nazis
4. Setting
5. Copenhagen fun spot, Tivoli _____
6. Trick to fool Nazis
7. Jewish friend of Annemarie
8. Copenhagen street
10. Kirsti's kitten; God of _____
15. How Mrs. Rosen felt in the boat
16. Courageous young Danish girl
17. Hid blankets and clothes
19. Borders Denmark to the west, _____ Sea

Number the Stars Crossword 1 Answer Key

						1 K				
2 P	3 R	I	4 D	E	5 G	I	6 R	A	7 F	8 F	E	O
	E		E		A		O		U	9 L	I	S	E
	S		N		R		N		N	L		T	
	I		M		D		E		E	E		E	10 T
	11 S	T	A	R	E		R		R	N		R	H
	T		R		N				A			B	U
	A		12 K	I	R	S	T	I	L		13 T	R	U	N	K
	N										O		D
14 C	H	R	15 I	S	T	16 I	A	N			G		E
	E		S			N					A		R
			E			N					D		
17 C			A		18 H	E	N	R	I	K	E		
O		19 N			I								
F		20 O	C	C	U	P	A	T	I	O	N		
F		R		K		R							
21 B	I	R	T	E		22 I	N	G	E	B	O	R	G
	N		H		23 G	O	N	E					

Across
- 2. Strong Jewish trait
- 5. Nickname for tall Nazi soldier
- 9. Older sister of Annemarie and Kirsti
- 11. Symbol of Jewish faith, _____ of David
- 12. Obstinate younger sister of Annemarie
- 13. Lise's trousseau is in it
- 14. Danish king, _____ the tenth
- 18. Fisherman who lives by the sea, Uncle_____
- 20. Nazi soldiers patrolling in Denmark, Nazi _____
- 21. Pretend dead aunt
- 22. Smuggled Jews out of Denmark
- 23. Mama's favorite story, _____ With The Wind

Down
- 1. Danish money
- 3. Worked secretly against Nazis
- 4. Setting
- 5. Copenhagen fun spot, Tivoli _____
- 6. Trick to fool Nazis
- 7. Jewish friend of Annemarie
- 8. Copenhagen street
- 10. Kirsti's kitten; God of _____
- 15. How Mrs. Rosen felt in the boat
- 16. Courageous young Danish girl
- 17. Hid blankets and clothes
- 19. Borders Denmark to the west, _____Sea

Number the Stars Crossword 2

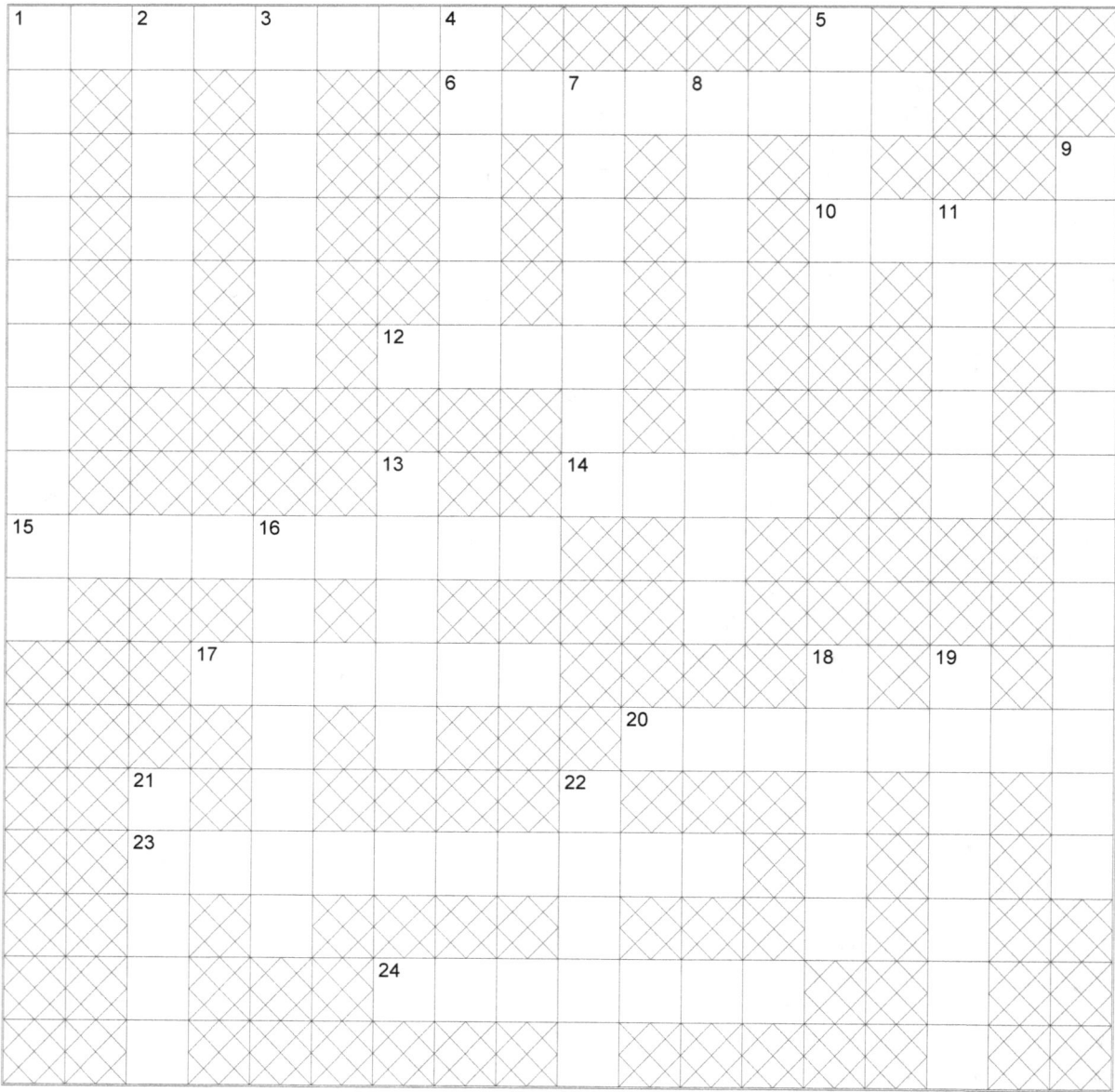

Across
1. Girls' bookbag
6. Smuggled Jews out of Denmark
10. Lise danced in it on her engagement, yellow _____
12. Older sister of Annemarie and Kirsti
14. Symbol of Jewish faith, _____ of David
15. Danish king, _____ the tenth
17. De Frie _____
20. Nazi symbol
23. Nazi soldiers patrolling in Denmark, Nazi _____
24. None is available during war

Down
1. Worked secretly against Nazis
2. Hid blankets and clothes
3. Jews were taken to this place by boat
4. Obstinate younger sister of Annemarie
5. Strong Jewish trait
7. Copenhagen fun spot, Tivoli _____
8. All of Denmark is King Christian's
9. Copenhagen street
11. Jewish friend of Annemarie
13. Button shop lady, Mrs. _____
16. How Mrs. Rosen felt in the boat
18. Contains words in title of book
19. Nickname for tall Nazi soldier
21. Borders Denmark to the west, _____ Sea
22. Pretend dead aunt

Number the Stars Crossword 2 Answer Key

	1 R	2 U	3 C	K	S	A	C	4 K			5 P		
	E	O		W				6 I	7 N	8 G	E	B	O	R	G
	S	F		E				R	A		O		I			9 O
	I	F		D				S	R		D		10 D	R	11 E	S	S
	S	I		E				T	D		Y		E		L		T
	T	N		N		12 L	I	S	E		G		L		L		E
	A								N		U				E		R
	N				13 H		14 S	T	A	R				N		B
15 C	H	R	16 I	S	T	I	A	N		R					R
E			S		E		R			D					O
		17 D	A	N	S	K	E				18 P		19 G	
			S		H			20 S	W	A	S	T	I	K	A
		21 N			I		22 B				A		R		D
		23 O	C	C	U	P	A	T	I	O	N		L		A	E
		R		K			R				M		F	
		T			24 L	E	A	T	H	E	R		F	
		H					E						E	

Across
1. Girls' bookbag
6. Smuggled Jews out of Denmark
10. Lise danced in it on her engagement, yellow _____
12. Older sister of Annemarie and Kirsti
14. Symbol of Jewish faith, _____ of David
15. Danish king, _____ the tenth
17. De Frie _____
20. Nazi symbol
23. Nazi soldiers patrolling in Denmark, Nazi _____
24. None is available during war

Down
1. Worked secretly against Nazis
2. Hid blankets and clothes
3. Jews were taken to this place by boat
4. Obstinate younger sister of Annemarie
5. Strong Jewish trait
7. Copenhagen fun spot, Tivoli _____
8. All of Denmark is King Christian's
9. Copenhagen street
11. Jewish friend of Annemarie
13. Button shop lady, Mrs. _____
16. How Mrs. Rosen felt in the boat
18. Contains words in title of book
19. Nickname for tall Nazi soldier
21. Borders Denmark to the west, _____ Sea
22. Pretend dead aunt

Number the Stars Crossword 3

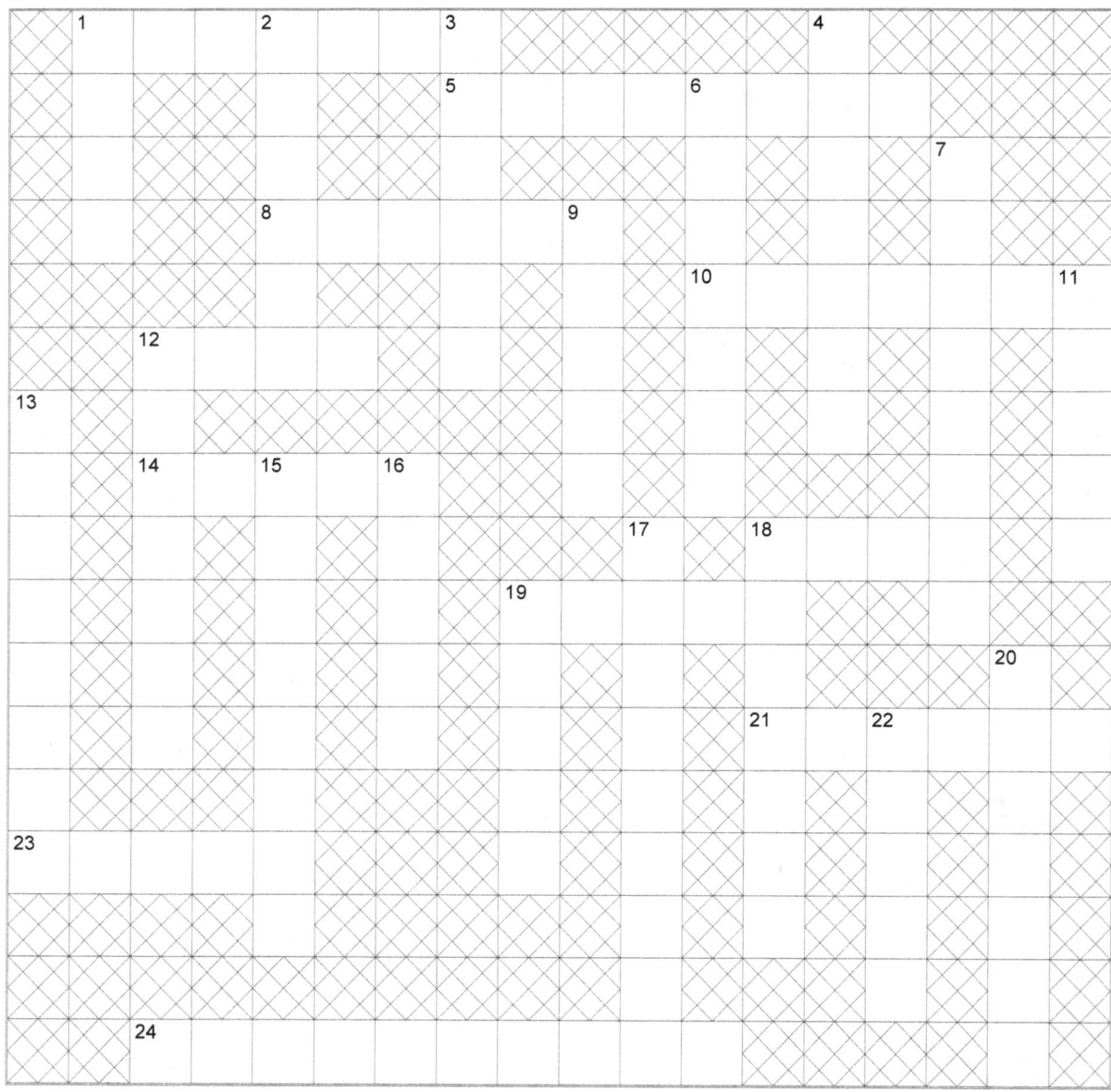

Across
1. How Mrs. Rosen felt in the boat
5. Smuggled Jews out of Denmark
8. De Frie _____
10. Nazi soldier did this to Mama
12. Mama's favorite story, _____ With The Wind
14. Jewish schoolteacher, Mr. _____
18. Older sister of Annemarie and Kirsti
19. Strong Jewish trait
21. Cause of Great Aunt Birte's death
23. Lise's trousseau is in it
24. Capital of Denmark

Down
1. Symbol of Jewish faith, _____ of David
2. Jews were taken to this place by boat
3. Obstinate younger sister of Annemarie
4. Fatihful dog of Mama's
6. Provided family with milk
7. Pink frosted ones were nowhere to be found
9. Jewish friend of Annemarie
11. Lise danced in it on her engagement, yellow _____
12. Copenhagen fun spot, Tivoli _____
13. North Sea channel between Sweden and Denmark
15. Nazi symbol
16. Borders Denmark to the west, _____ Sea
17. Coast of Denmark near Sweden
18. None is available during war
19. Red-headed fiance of Lise
20. King Christian's faithful horse
22. Contains words in title of book

Number the Stars Crossword 3 Answer Key

	1 S	E	2 A	S	3 I	C	K				4 T			
	T		W		5 I	N	G	E	6 B	O	R	G		
	A		E		R				L		O		7 C	
	R		8 D	A	N	S	K	9 E			F		U	
			E		T			L		10 S	L	A	P	P	E	11 D
		12 G	O	N	E			L		S		S		C		R
13 K		A						E		S		T		A		E
A		14 R	O	15 S	E	16 N		N		M				K		S
T		D		W		O			17 G		18 L	I	S	E		S
T		E		A		R		19 P	R	I	D	E		S		
E		N		S		T		E			L		A		20 J	
G		S		T		H		T		21 T	Y	22 P	H	U	S	
A				I				E		H		S			B	
23 T	R	U	N	K				R		L		E			I	
				A				E		E		R			L	
								E		R		L			L	
								J				M			E	
		24 C	O	P	E	N	H	A	G	E	N				E	

Across
1. How Mrs. Rosen felt in the boat
5. Smuggled Jews out of Denmark
8. De Frie _____
10. Nazi soldier did this to Mama
12. Mama's favorite story, _____ With The Wind
14. Jewish schoolteacher, Mr. _____
18. Older sister of Annemarie and Kirsti
19. Strong Jewish trait
21. Cause of Great Aunt Birte's death
23. Lise's trousseau is in it
24. Capital of Denmark

Down
1. Symbol of Jewish faith, _____ of David
2. Jews were taken to this place by boat
3. Obstinate younger sister of Annemarie
4. Fatiful dog of Mama's
6. Provided family with milk
7. Pink frosted ones were nowhere to be found
9. Jewish friend of Annemarie
11. Lise danced in it on her engagement, yellow _____
12. Copenhagen fun spot, Tivoli _____
13. North Sea channel between Sweden and Denmark
15. Nazi symbol
16. Borders Denmark to the west, _____ Sea
17. Coast of Denmark near Sweden
18. None is available during war
19. Red-headed fiance of Lise
20. King Christian's faithful horse
22. Contains words in title of book

Number the Stars Crossword 4

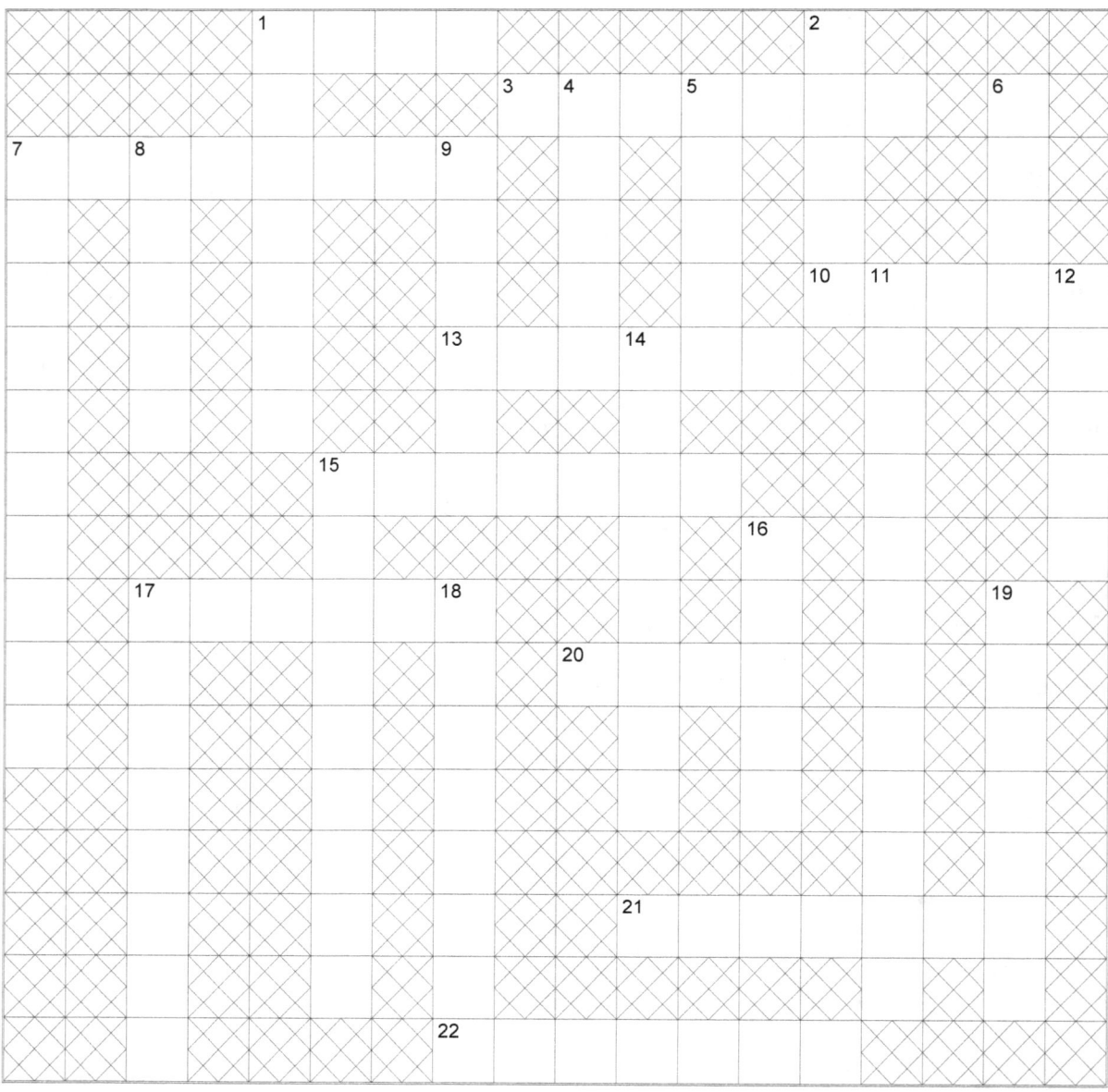

Across
1. Symbol of Jewish faith, _____ of David
3. None is available during war
7. Pink frosted ones were nowhere to be found
10. Jewish schoolteacher, Mr. _____
13. De Frie _____
15. Trick to fool Nazis
17. Obstinate younger sister of Annemarie
20. Older sister of Annemarie and Kirsti
21. Kirsti's kitten; God of _____
22. Copenhagen fun spot, Tivoli _____

Down
1. How Mrs. Rosen felt in the boat
2. Red-headed fiance of Lise
4. Jewish friend of Annemarie
5. Lise's trousseau is in it
6. Mama's favorite story, _____ With The Wind
7. Capital of Denmark
8. Strong Jewish trait
9. Jews were taken to this place by boat
11. Copenhagen street
12. Borders Denmark to the west, _____ Sea
14. Nazi symbol
15. Kirsti refused to wear
16. Lise danced in it on her engagement, yellow _____
17. North Sea channel between Sweden and Denmark
18. Smuggled Jews out of Denmark
19. Setting

Number the Stars Crossword 4 Answer Key

			1 S	T	A	R				2 P			
			E			3 L	4 E	5 A	T	H	E	R	6 G
7 C	U	8 P	C	A	K	E	S	9 L		R		T	O
O		R		S			W	L		L		E	N
P		I					E	E		N		10 R	11 O	S	12 E	N
E		D		C		13 D	A	14 N	S	K	E		S			O
N		E		K		E		W					T			R
H				15 F	U	N	E	R	A	L			E			T
A					I			S		16 D		R			H
G	17 K	I	R	S	T	18 I		T		R		B		19 D
E	A				H		N		20 L	I	S	E		R			E
N	T				S		G		K			S		R			N
	T				H		E		A			S		G			M
	E				O		B							A			A
	G				E		O		21 T	H	U	N	D	E	R
	A				S		R							E			K
	T						22 G	A	R	D	E	N	S	

Across
1. Symbol of Jewish faith, _____ of David
3. None is available during war
7. Pink frosted ones were nowhere to be found
10. Jewish schoolteacher, Mr. _____
13. De Frie _____
15. Trick to fool Nazis
17. Obstinate younger sister of Annemarie
20. Older sister of Annemarie and Kirsti
21. Kirsti's kitten; God of _____
22. Copenhagen fun spot, Tivoli _____

Down
1. How Mrs. Rosen felt in the boat
2. Red-headed fiance of Lise
4. Jewish friend of Annemarie
5. Lise's trousseau is in it
6. Mama's favorite story, _____ With The Wind
7. Capital of Denmark
8. Strong Jewish trait
9. Jews were taken to this place by boat
11. Copenhagen street
12. Borders Denmark to the west, _____ Sea
14. Nazi symbol
15. Kirsti refused to wear
16. Lise danced in it on her engagement, yellow _____
17. North Sea channel between Sweden and Denmark
18. Smuggled Jews out of Denmark
19. Setting

Number the Stars

KIRSTI	BIRTE	PHOTOGRAPH	TRUNK	PRIDE
HENRIK	COFFIN	DANSKE	INGEBORG	FISH SHOES
BODYGUARD	HOLOCAUST	FREE SPACE	LEATHER	LISE
KATTEGAT	SWASTIKA	ANNEMARIE	BLOSSOM	GIRAFFE
JUBILEE	DENMARK	DRUNKARD	FUNERAL	TYPHUS

Number the Stars

HIRSH	SPECIAL	DRESS	FIREWORKS	CROCHETING
LOWRY	COPENHAGEN	TROFAST	GARDENS	AMALIENBORG
ROSEN	THUNDER	FREE SPACE	HANDKERCHIEF	SWEDEN
STAR	BALTIC	SEASICK	SLAPPED	OSTERBROGADE
CHRISTIAN	GONE	ANDERSON	RUCKSACK	ELLEN

Number the Stars

BIRTE	DRUNKARD	STAR	DANSKE	ANNEMARIE
TRUNK	DENMARK	TROFAST	HOLOCAUST	BALTIC
RESISTANCE	PETER	FREE SPACE	JUBILEE	FIREWORKS
PRIDE	CUPCAKES	OSTERBROGADE	HANDKERCHIEF	BLOSSOM
SWASTIKA	ROSEN	NORTH	PSALM	COFFIN

Number the Stars

SEASICK	LOWRY	TYPHUS	SPECIAL	ANDERSON
INGEBORG	SWEDEN	FUNERAL	GONE	BODYGUARD
OCCUPATION	SLAPPED	FREE SPACE	CHRISTIAN	RUCKSACK
ELLEN	COPENHAGEN	FISH SHOES	GIRAFFE	DRESS
PHOTOGRAPH	GARDENS	CROCHETING	GILLELEJE	KATTEGAT

Number the Stars

HANDKERCHIEF	COPENHAGEN	DANSKE	CROCHETING	FUNERAL
INGEBORG	RUCKSACK	JUBILEE	TROFAST	BODYGUARD
GONE	NORTH	FREE SPACE	SWEDEN	AMALIENBORG
TRUNK	ELLEN	BALTIC	PETER	KATTEGAT
SWASTIKA	OCCUPATION	HENRIK	ANDERSON	SEASICK

Number the Stars

GIRAFFE	KRONER	SLAPPED	GILLELEJE	DENMARK
THUNDER	PHOTOGRAPH	TYPHUS	DRUNKARD	KIRSTI
HIRSH	RESISTANCE	FREE SPACE	FISH SHOES	SPECIAL
ROSEN	LEATHER	BLOSSOM	CHRISTIAN	STAR
LISE	PSALM	COFFIN	LOWRY	PRIDE

Number the Stars

GILLELEJE	INGEBORG	OSTERBROGADE	ANDERSON	LEATHER
DRUNKARD	DRESS	LISE	THUNDER	FIREWORKS
SWEDEN	HENRIK	FREE SPACE	BLOSSOM	ROSEN
STAR	ANNEMARIE	RUCKSACK	ELLEN	COFFIN
PHOTOGRAPH	NORTH	TROFAST	CROCHETING	CHRISTIAN

Number the Stars

BODYGUARD	PETER	KRONER	FUNERAL	HOLOCAUST
KIRSTI	HIRSH	TYPHUS	GARDENS	DENMARK
AMALIENBORG	KATTEGAT	FREE SPACE	BALTIC	SLAPPED
CUPCAKES	BIRTE	TRUNK	LOWRY	SEASICK
GIRAFFE	FISH SHOES	HANDKERCHIEF	SWASTIKA	PRIDE

Number the Stars

ELLEN	JUBILEE	RUCKSACK	COFFIN	AMALIENBORG
BIRTE	GARDENS	BODYGUARD	PHOTOGRAPH	LISE
GONE	HANDKERCHIEF	FREE SPACE	BALTIC	SWEDEN
PRIDE	DENMARK	ROSEN	DRUNKARD	CUPCAKES
OCCUPATION	BLOSSOM	LOWRY	DRESS	THUNDER

Number the Stars

ANNEMARIE	COPENHAGEN	HENRIK	TROFAST	CHRISTIAN
KIRSTI	PSALM	TRUNK	PETER	FUNERAL
SWASTIKA	GIRAFFE	FREE SPACE	LEATHER	HOLOCAUST
DANSKE	TYPHUS	CROCHETING	NORTH	RESISTANCE
ANDERSON	STAR	SPECIAL	INGEBORG	SLAPPED

Number the Stars

HENRIK	SWEDEN	CROCHETING	SLAPPED	STAR
CUPCAKES	KIRSTI	GIRAFFE	ANNEMARIE	DANSKE
HIRSH	JUBILEE	FREE SPACE	FISH SHOES	ANDERSON
BLOSSOM	SPECIAL	RUCKSACK	PHOTOGRAPH	GARDENS
PSALM	SEASICK	INGEBORG	OCCUPATION	LOWRY

Number the Stars

ELLEN	SWASTIKA	BODYGUARD	THUNDER	DRESS
GILLELEJE	RESISTANCE	OSTERBROGADE	LEATHER	BALTIC
KRONER	DENMARK	FREE SPACE	COFFIN	ROSEN
CHRISTIAN	TROFAST	COPENHAGEN	TYPHUS	AMALIENBORG
GONE	PRIDE	TRUNK	KATTEGAT	BIRTE

Number the Stars

SLAPPED	FUNERAL	PHOTOGRAPH	HENRIK	DENMARK
FISH SHOES	HOLOCAUST	DRUNKARD	ROSEN	CUPCAKES
RUCKSACK	LEATHER	FREE SPACE	CROCHETING	TROFAST
PRIDE	SWASTIKA	ELLEN	THUNDER	SWEDEN
LOWRY	PETER	KATTEGAT	GONE	GARDENS

Number the Stars

LISE	DRESS	HIRSH	SEASICK	TRUNK
OSTERBROGADE	BLOSSOM	PSALM	GILLELEJE	STAR
TYPHUS	NORTH	FREE SPACE	SPECIAL	ANDERSON
BALTIC	COPENHAGEN	DANSKE	KIRSTI	HANDKERCHIEF
BODYGUARD	AMALIENBORG	INGEBORG	COFFIN	ANNEMARIE

Number the Stars

COPENHAGEN	COFFIN	HANDKERCHIEF	KRONER	ROSEN
BIRTE	NORTH	TROFAST	BALTIC	LEATHER
DRESS	GARDENS	FREE SPACE	OSTERBROGADE	SWEDEN
SEASICK	BLOSSOM	PHOTOGRAPH	ANDERSON	LISE
LOWRY	RUCKSACK	STAR	PSALM	HENRIK

Number the Stars

AMALIENBORG	CROCHETING	DRUNKARD	DENMARK	RESISTANCE
GIRAFFE	KATTEGAT	INGEBORG	GONE	TRUNK
FUNERAL	HOLOCAUST	FREE SPACE	KIRSTI	OCCUPATION
SLAPPED	TYPHUS	DANSKE	GILLELEJE	PETER
PRIDE	CUPCAKES	BODYGUARD	THUNDER	SPECIAL

Number the Stars

FUNERAL	BALTIC	RUCKSACK	LOWRY	PETER
BODYGUARD	RESISTANCE	CUPCAKES	LEATHER	BIRTE
FIREWORKS	CROCHETING	FREE SPACE	GARDENS	HANDKERCHIEF
PSALM	LISE	COPENHAGEN	OCCUPATION	DENMARK
HOLOCAUST	KRONER	GIRAFFE	SLAPPED	ANNEMARIE

Number the Stars

AMALIENBORG	TYPHUS	SEASICK	HIRSH	ANDERSON
GONE	NORTH	SWEDEN	BLOSSOM	DANSKE
STAR	TRUNK	FREE SPACE	TROFAST	KATTEGAT
FISH SHOES	ROSEN	ELLEN	JUBILEE	GILLELEJE
THUNDER	DRESS	SPECIAL	PRIDE	PHOTOGRAPH

Number the Stars

DANSKE	STAR	SWASTIKA	CUPCAKES	DRESS
FUNERAL	TYPHUS	OCCUPATION	INGEBORG	FIREWORKS
FISH SHOES	CROCHETING	FREE SPACE	KATTEGAT	BIRTE
HENRIK	SWEDEN	ROSEN	ANDERSON	GARDENS
CHRISTIAN	PHOTOGRAPH	LEATHER	ELLEN	OSTERBROGADE

Number the Stars

PETER	HANDKERCHIEF	JUBILEE	BLOSSOM	PRIDE
RUCKSACK	LISE	COPENHAGEN	GILLELEJE	TROFAST
DENMARK	KIRSTI	FREE SPACE	GONE	LOWRY
GIRAFFE	KRONER	RESISTANCE	AMALIENBORG	DRUNKARD
NORTH	SEASICK	BODYGUARD	SLAPPED	SPECIAL

Number the Stars

HENRIK	GONE	DENMARK	PHOTOGRAPH	LISE
THUNDER	FISH SHOES	SLAPPED	PSALM	BIRTE
ANNEMARIE	LOWRY	FREE SPACE	DRUNKARD	RUCKSACK
CUPCAKES	CROCHETING	ROSEN	SEASICK	SPECIAL
CHRISTIAN	TYPHUS	SWASTIKA	TRUNK	HANDKERCHIEF

Number the Stars

KIRSTI	KATTEGAT	OSTERBROGADE	FUNERAL	PRIDE
COFFIN	SWEDEN	BODYGUARD	HIRSH	ANDERSON
OCCUPATION	PETER	FREE SPACE	BALTIC	STAR
GARDENS	BLOSSOM	GIRAFFE	ELLEN	INGEBORG
LEATHER	GILLELEJE	COPENHAGEN	DRESS	TROFAST

Number the Stars

GILLELEJE	PSALM	FIREWORKS	OCCUPATION	COFFIN
PRIDE	RUCKSACK	CHRISTIAN	TROFAST	COPENHAGEN
STAR	DRUNKARD	FREE SPACE	PHOTOGRAPH	ELLEN
ANNEMARIE	BIRTE	CROCHETING	GARDENS	SPECIAL
NORTH	ANDERSON	GIRAFFE	JUBILEE	ROSEN

Number the Stars

GONE	HIRSH	KATTEGAT	INGEBORG	PETER
SEASICK	THUNDER	OSTERBROGADE	HANDKERCHIEF	SLAPPED
HENRIK	RESISTANCE	FREE SPACE	BALTIC	FISH SHOES
LISE	KIRSTI	KRONER	SWEDEN	AMALIENBORG
BODYGUARD	BLOSSOM	HOLOCAUST	CUPCAKES	SWASTIKA

Number the Stars

FIREWORKS	HANDKERCHIEF	FUNERAL	COPENHAGEN	PHOTOGRAPH
PSALM	LISE	OSTERBROGADE	BALTIC	SWEDEN
LEATHER	CROCHETING	FREE SPACE	DRESS	PETER
HIRSH	GARDENS	LOWRY	KIRSTI	GIRAFFE
COFFIN	FISH SHOES	PRIDE	OCCUPATION	RUCKSACK

Number the Stars

DANSKE	TYPHUS	SWASTIKA	ANNEMARIE	THUNDER
JUBILEE	DRUNKARD	ROSEN	BODYGUARD	ANDERSON
BIRTE	STAR	FREE SPACE	KATTEGAT	CUPCAKES
TRUNK	HENRIK	RESISTANCE	NORTH	AMALIENBORG
GONE	ELLEN	DENMARK	GILLELEJE	HOLOCAUST

Number the Stars

BLOSSOM	DRESS	PETER	PHOTOGRAPH	KIRSTI
RESISTANCE	AMALIENBORG	SLAPPED	SWASTIKA	NORTH
FIREWORKS	BODYGUARD	FREE SPACE	TYPHUS	SWEDEN
OSTERBROGADE	HIRSH	CUPCAKES	DANSKE	ANDERSON
FUNERAL	DENMARK	LOWRY	TRUNK	INGEBORG

Number the Stars

LEATHER	KATTEGAT	PSALM	DRUNKARD	COPENHAGEN
HANDKERCHIEF	COFFIN	ROSEN	CROCHETING	HENRIK
GILLELEJE	GONE	FREE SPACE	BIRTE	GARDENS
HOLOCAUST	THUNDER	LISE	ELLEN	SPECIAL
STAR	OCCUPATION	SEASICK	RUCKSACK	TROFAST

Number the Stars

SPECIAL	ELLEN	COPENHAGEN	JUBILEE	BLOSSOM
GONE	LISE	STAR	PETER	ANNEMARIE
BODYGUARD	GILLELEJE	FREE SPACE	HENRIK	TRUNK
FISH SHOES	PRIDE	COFFIN	PHOTOGRAPH	HANDKERCHIEF
CUPCAKES	FUNERAL	DRESS	NORTH	SWEDEN

Number the Stars

TYPHUS	GIRAFFE	CROCHETING	HOLOCAUST	SLAPPED
AMALIENBORG	LEATHER	KRONER	OSTERBROGADE	BALTIC
KATTEGAT	GARDENS	FREE SPACE	PSALM	FIREWORKS
BIRTE	ANDERSON	TROFAST	RESISTANCE	HIRSH
THUNDER	LOWRY	RUCKSACK	OCCUPATION	INGEBORG

Number the Stars

SEASICK	KATTEGAT	PSALM	ANNEMARIE	HIRSH
SLAPPED	ANDERSON	PETER	GIRAFFE	DENMARK
DRUNKARD	COPENHAGEN	FREE SPACE	HANDKERCHIEF	PHOTOGRAPH
TRUNK	NORTH	STAR	OCCUPATION	COFFIN
ROSEN	BLOSSOM	LISE	TYPHUS	BODYGUARD

Number the Stars

SPECIAL	FUNERAL	BALTIC	HOLOCAUST	JUBILEE
SWASTIKA	HENRIK	DANSKE	PRIDE	GONE
THUNDER	ELLEN	FREE SPACE	GARDENS	KRONER
INGEBORG	RESISTANCE	RUCKSACK	CUPCAKES	KIRSTI
DRESS	OSTERBROGADE	LEATHER	GILLELEJE	TROFAST

Number the Stars Vocabulary Word List

No.	Word	Clue/Definition
1.	BELLIGERENTLY	IN A HOSTILE MANNER
2.	CONTEMPT	DISGUST; DISTASTE
3.	CROCHETING	NEEDLEWORK SIMILAR TO KNITTING
4.	DEFIANTLY	BOLDLY; REBELLIOUSLY
5.	DESIGNATED	APPOINTED
6.	DISDAINFULLY	SCORNFULLY
7.	DUBIOUSLY	DOUBTFULLY
8.	EMBROIDERED	DECORATED WITH NEEDLEWORK
9.	EXASPERATED	ANNOYED; IRRITATED
10.	HAUGHTILY	ARROGANTLY; HIGH AND MIGHTILY
11.	HOODLUMS	CRIMINALS; HOOLIGANS
12.	IMPASSIVE	UNEMOTIONAL; INDIFFERENT
13.	IMPERIOUS	DOMINEERING; OVERBEARING
14.	IMPRINTED	PRESSED INTO
15.	INTONED	RECITED; SPOKE
16.	INTRICATE	DETAILED
17.	LANKY	LEAN; THIN
18.	OBSTINATE	STUBBORN
19.	RABBI	JEWISH MINISTER
20.	RESIDENTIAL	AREA WHERE HOMES ARE LOCATED
21.	SABBATH	HOLY DAY
22.	SABOTAGE	VANDALIZE
23.	SARCASTICALLY	IN A CUTTING MANNER
24.	SOPHISTICATED	CULTURED; REFINED
25.	SUBMERGED	PLUNGED UNDERWATER
26.	SYNAGOGUE	JEWISH CHURCH
27.	TROUSSEAU	ITEMS BROUGHT TO MARRIAGE BY BRIDE
28.	TRUDGED	PLODDED; MARCHED
29.	UNWAVERING	STABLE; STEADY

Number the Stars Vocabulary Fill In The Blank 1

_____ 1. IN A HOSTILE MANNER

_____ 2. STABLE; STEADY

_____ 3. LEAN; THIN

_____ 4. DETAILED

_____ 5. ANNOYED; IRRITATED

_____ 6. DOUBTFULLY

_____ 7. BOLDLY; REBELLIOUSLY

_____ 8. NEEDLEWORK SIMILAR TO KNITTING

_____ 9. UNEMOTIONAL; INDIFFERENT

_____ 10. ITEMS BROUGHT TO MARRIAGE BY BRIDE

_____ 11. HOLY DAY

_____ 12. PLUNGED UNDERWATER

_____ 13. DOMINEERING; OVERBEARING

_____ 14. STUBBORN

_____ 15. ARROGANTLY; HIGH AND MIGHTILY

_____ 16. DISGUST; DISTASTE

_____ 17. JEWISH MINISTER

_____ 18. PRESSED INTO

_____ 19. SCORNFULLY

_____ 20. DECORATED WITH NEEDLEWORK

Number the Stars Vocabulary Fill In The Blank 1 Answer Key

BELLIGERENTLY	1. IN A HOSTILE MANNER
UNWAVERING	2. STABLE; STEADY
LANKY	3. LEAN; THIN
INTRICATE	4. DETAILED
EXASPERATED	5. ANNOYED; IRRITATED
DUBIOUSLY	6. DOUBTFULLY
DEFIANTLY	7. BOLDLY; REBELLIOUSLY
CROCHETING	8. NEEDLEWORK SIMILAR TO KNITTING
IMPASSIVE	9. UNEMOTIONAL; INDIFFERENT
TROUSSEAU	10. ITEMS BROUGHT TO MARRIAGE BY BRIDE
SABBATH	11. HOLY DAY
SUBMERGED	12. PLUNGED UNDERWATER
IMPERIOUS	13. DOMINEERING; OVERBEARING
OBSTINATE	14. STUBBORN
HAUGHTILY	15. ARROGANTLY; HIGH AND MIGHTILY
CONTEMPT	16. DISGUST; DISTASTE
RABBI	17. JEWISH MINISTER
IMPRINTED	18. PRESSED INTO
DISDAINFULLY	19. SCORNFULLY
EMBROIDERED	20. DECORATED WITH NEEDLEWORK

Number the Stars Vocabulary Fill In The Blank 2

_____ 1. SCORNFULLY

_____ 2. ANNOYED; IRRITATED

_____ 3. CULTURED; REFINED

_____ 4. UNEMOTIONAL; INDIFFERENT

_____ 5. CRIMINALS; HOOLIGANS

_____ 6. LEAN; THIN

_____ 7. NEEDLEWORK SIMILAR TO KNITTING

_____ 8. DETAILED

_____ 9. DISGUST; DISTASTE

_____ 10. DOUBTFULLY

_____ 11. PRESSED INTO

_____ 12. JEWISH CHURCH

_____ 13. PLUNGED UNDERWATER

_____ 14. STABLE; STEADY

_____ 15. BOLDLY; REBELLIOUSLY

_____ 16. PLODDED; MARCHED

_____ 17. RECITED; SPOKE

_____ 18. IN A HOSTILE MANNER

_____ 19. ARROGANTLY; HIGH AND MIGHTILY

_____ 20. ITEMS BROUGHT TO MARRIAGE BY BRIDE

Number the Stars Vocabulary Fill In The Blank 2 Answer Key

DISDAINFULLY	1. SCORNFULLY
EXASPERATED	2. ANNOYED; IRRITATED
SOPHISTICATED	3. CULTURED; REFINED
IMPASSIVE	4. UNEMOTIONAL; INDIFFERENT
HOODLUMS	5. CRIMINALS; HOOLIGANS
LANKY	6. LEAN; THIN
CROCHETING	7. NEEDLEWORK SIMILAR TO KNITTING
INTRICATE	8. DETAILED
CONTEMPT	9. DISGUST; DISTASTE
DUBIOUSLY	10. DOUBTFULLY
IMPRINTED	11. PRESSED INTO
SYNAGOGUE	12. JEWISH CHURCH
SUBMERGED	13. PLUNGED UNDERWATER
UNWAVERING	14. STABLE; STEADY
DEFIANTLY	15. BOLDLY; REBELLIOUSLY
TRUDGED	16. PLODDED; MARCHED
INTONED	17. RECITED; SPOKE
BELLIGERENTLY	18. IN A HOSTILE MANNER
HAUGHTILY	19. ARROGANTLY; HIGH AND MIGHTILY
TROUSSEAU	20. ITEMS BROUGHT TO MARRIAGE BY BRIDE

Copyrighted

Number the Stars Vocabulary Fill In The Blank 3

_____ 1. JEWISH MINISTER

_____ 2. ANNOYED; IRRITATED

_____ 3. ITEMS BROUGHT TO MARRIAGE BY BRIDE

_____ 4. DOUBTFULLY

_____ 5. JEWISH CHURCH

_____ 6. RECITED; SPOKE

_____ 7. CRIMINALS; HOOLIGANS

_____ 8. DOMINEERING; OVERBEARING

_____ 9. LEAN; THIN

_____ 10. STUBBORN

_____ 11. DISGUST; DISTASTE

_____ 12. ARROGANTLY; HIGH AND MIGHTILY

_____ 13. AREA WHERE HOMES ARE LOCATED

_____ 14. DECORATED WITH NEEDLEWORK

_____ 15. PLUNGED UNDERWATER

_____ 16. CULTURED; REFINED

_____ 17. NEEDLEWORK SIMILAR TO KNITTING

_____ 18. VANDALIZE

_____ 19. STABLE; STEADY

_____ 20. PLODDED; MARCHED

Number the Stars Vocabulary Fill In The Blank 3 Answer Key

RABBI	1. JEWISH MINISTER
EXASPERATED	2. ANNOYED; IRRITATED
TROUSSEAU	3. ITEMS BROUGHT TO MARRIAGE BY BRIDE
DUBIOUSLY	4. DOUBTFULLY
SYNAGOGUE	5. JEWISH CHURCH
INTONED	6. RECITED; SPOKE
HOODLUMS	7. CRIMINALS; HOOLIGANS
IMPERIOUS	8. DOMINEERING; OVERBEARING
LANKY	9. LEAN; THIN
OBSTINATE	10. STUBBORN
CONTEMPT	11. DISGUST; DISTASTE
HAUGHTILY	12. ARROGANTLY; HIGH AND MIGHTILY
RESIDENTIAL	13. AREA WHERE HOMES ARE LOCATED
EMBROIDERED	14. DECORATED WITH NEEDLEWORK
SUBMERGED	15. PLUNGED UNDERWATER
SOPHISTICATED	16. CULTURED; REFINED
CROCHETING	17. NEEDLEWORK SIMILAR TO KNITTING
SABOTAGE	18. VANDALIZE
UNWAVERING	19. STABLE; STEADY
TRUDGED	20. PLODDED; MARCHED

Number the Stars Vocabulary Fill In The Blank 4

_____ 1. LEAN; THIN

_____ 2. HOLY DAY

_____ 3. NEEDLEWORK SIMILAR TO KNITTING

_____ 4. ITEMS BROUGHT TO MARRIAGE BY BRIDE

_____ 5. IN A HOSTILE MANNER

_____ 6. VANDALIZE

_____ 7. JEWISH MINISTER

_____ 8. PRESSED INTO

_____ 9. RECITED; SPOKE

_____ 10. DOMINEERING; OVERBEARING

_____ 11. UNEMOTIONAL; INDIFFERENT

_____ 12. CRIMINALS; HOOLIGANS

_____ 13. DOUBTFULLY

_____ 14. SCORNFULLY

_____ 15. CULTURED; REFINED

_____ 16. IN A CUTTING MANNER

_____ 17. PLUNGED UNDERWATER

_____ 18. STUBBORN

_____ 19. DETAILED

_____ 20. DECORATED WITH NEEDLEWORK

Number the Stars Vocabulary Fill In The Blank 4 Answer Key

LANKY	1. LEAN; THIN
SABBATH	2. HOLY DAY
CROCHETING	3. NEEDLEWORK SIMILAR TO KNITTING
TROUSSEAU	4. ITEMS BROUGHT TO MARRIAGE BY BRIDE
BELLIGERENTLY	5. IN A HOSTILE MANNER
SABOTAGE	6. VANDALIZE
RABBI	7. JEWISH MINISTER
IMPRINTED	8. PRESSED INTO
INTONED	9. RECITED; SPOKE
IMPERIOUS	10. DOMINEERING; OVERBEARING
IMPASSIVE	11. UNEMOTIONAL; INDIFFERENT
HOODLUMS	12. CRIMINALS; HOOLIGANS
DUBIOUSLY	13. DOUBTFULLY
DISDAINFULLY	14. SCORNFULLY
SOPHISTICATED	15. CULTURED; REFINED
SARCASTICALLY	16. IN A CUTTING MANNER
SUBMERGED	17. PLUNGED UNDERWATER
OBSTINATE	18. STUBBORN
INTRICATE	19. DETAILED
EMBROIDERED	20. DECORATED WITH NEEDLEWORK

Number the Stars Vocabulary Matching 1

___ 1. INTRICATE
___ 2. HOODLUMS
___ 3. HAUGHTILY
___ 4. DISDAINFULLY
___ 5. TROUSSEAU
___ 6. EXASPERATED
___ 7. SYNAGOGUE
___ 8. TRUDGED
___ 9. SABOTAGE
___ 10. IMPASSIVE
___ 11. DESIGNATED
___ 12. DUBIOUSLY
___ 13. UNWAVERING
___ 14. SOPHISTICATED
___ 15. SUBMERGED
___ 16. CROCHETING
___ 17. BELLIGERENTLY
___ 18. IMPRINTED
___ 19. DEFIANTLY
___ 20. SARCASTICALLY
___ 21. CONTEMPT
___ 22. SABBATH
___ 23. LANKY
___ 24. IMPERIOUS
___ 25. OBSTINATE

A. IN A HOSTILE MANNER
B. CRIMINALS; HOOLIGANS
C. NEEDLEWORK SIMILAR TO KNITTING
D. PLODDED; MARCHED
E. VANDALIZE
F. STABLE; STEADY
G. ITEMS BROUGHT TO MARRIAGE BY BRIDE
H. DOMINEERING; OVERBEARING
I. PRESSED INTO
J. ANNOYED; IRRITATED
K. CULTURED; REFINED
L. UNEMOTIONAL; INDIFFERENT
M. DETAILED
N. HOLY DAY
O. DOUBTFULLY
P. DISGUST; DISTASTE
Q. BOLDLY; REBELLIOUSLY
R. JEWISH CHURCH
S. ARROGANTLY; HIGH AND MIGHTILY
T. SCORNFULLY
U. STUBBORN
V. PLUNGED UNDERWATER
W. IN A CUTTING MANNER
X. APPOINTED
Y. LEAN; THIN

Number the Stars Vocabulary Matching 1 Answer Key

M - 1.	INTRICATE	A. IN A HOSTILE MANNER
B - 2.	HOODLUMS	B. CRIMINALS; HOOLIGANS
S - 3.	HAUGHTILY	C. NEEDLEWORK SIMILAR TO KNITTING
T - 4.	DISDAINFULLY	D. PLODDED; MARCHED
G - 5.	TROUSSEAU	E. VANDALIZE
J - 6.	EXASPERATED	F. STABLE; STEADY
R - 7.	SYNAGOGUE	G. ITEMS BROUGHT TO MARRIAGE BY BRIDE
D - 8.	TRUDGED	H. DOMINEERING; OVERBEARING
E - 9.	SABOTAGE	I. PRESSED INTO
L - 10.	IMPASSIVE	J. ANNOYED; IRRITATED
X - 11.	DESIGNATED	K. CULTURED; REFINED
O - 12.	DUBIOUSLY	L. UNEMOTIONAL; INDIFFERENT
F - 13.	UNWAVERING	M. DETAILED
K - 14.	SOPHISTICATED	N. HOLY DAY
V - 15.	SUBMERGED	O. DOUBTFULLY
C - 16.	CROCHETING	P. DISGUST; DISTASTE
A - 17.	BELLIGERENTLY	Q. BOLDLY; REBELLIOUSLY
I - 18.	IMPRINTED	R. JEWISH CHURCH
Q - 19.	DEFIANTLY	S. ARROGANTLY; HIGH AND MIGHTILY
W - 20.	SARCASTICALLY	T. SCORNFULLY
P - 21.	CONTEMPT	U. STUBBORN
N - 22.	SABBATH	V. PLUNGED UNDERWATER
Y - 23.	LANKY	W. IN A CUTTING MANNER
H - 24.	IMPERIOUS	X. APPOINTED
U - 25.	OBSTINATE	Y. LEAN; THIN

Number the Stars Vocabulary Matching 2

___ 1. SYNAGOGUE   A. DISGUST; DISTASTE
___ 2. IMPASSIVE   B. STUBBORN
___ 3. DUBIOUSLY   C. UNEMOTIONAL; INDIFFERENT
___ 4. HOODLUMS   D. DOUBTFULLY
___ 5. CROCHETING   E. DOMINEERING; OVERBEARING
___ 6. SOPHISTICATED   F. ARROGANTLY; HIGH AND MIGHTILY
___ 7. EMBROIDERED   G. PLUNGED UNDERWATER
___ 8. IMPERIOUS   H. STABLE; STEADY
___ 9. DISDAINFULLY   I. JEWISH CHURCH
___10. SABOTAGE   J. ITEMS BROUGHT TO MARRIAGE BY BRIDE
___11. INTONED   K. DECORATED WITH NEEDLEWORK
___12. INTRICATE   L. BOLDLY; REBELLIOUSLY
___13. OBSTINATE   M. HOLY DAY
___14. HAUGHTILY   N. AREA WHERE HOMES ARE LOCATED
___15. UNWAVERING   O. DETAILED
___16. TROUSSEAU   P. CULTURED; REFINED
___17. SABBATH   Q. ANNOYED; IRRITATED
___18. SARCASTICALLY   R. IN A CUTTING MANNER
___19. RESIDENTIAL   S. NEEDLEWORK SIMILAR TO KNITTING
___20. EXASPERATED   T. VANDALIZE
___21. DEFIANTLY   U. RECITED; SPOKE
___22. TRUDGED   V. APPOINTED
___23. CONTEMPT   W. SCORNFULLY
___24. SUBMERGED   X. PLODDED; MARCHED
___25. DESIGNATED   Y. CRIMINALS; HOOLIGANS

Number the Stars Vocabulary Matching 2 Answer Key

I - 1. SYNAGOGUE	A.	DISGUST; DISTASTE
C - 2. IMPASSIVE	B.	STUBBORN
D - 3. DUBIOUSLY	C.	UNEMOTIONAL; INDIFFERENT
Y - 4. HOODLUMS	D.	DOUBTFULLY
S - 5. CROCHETING	E.	DOMINEERING; OVERBEARING
P - 6. SOPHISTICATED	F.	ARROGANTLY; HIGH AND MIGHTILY
K - 7. EMBROIDERED	G.	PLUNGED UNDERWATER
E - 8. IMPERIOUS	H.	STABLE; STEADY
W - 9. DISDAINFULLY	I.	JEWISH CHURCH
T - 10. SABOTAGE	J.	ITEMS BROUGHT TO MARRIAGE BY BRIDE
U - 11. INTONED	K.	DECORATED WITH NEEDLEWORK
O - 12. INTRICATE	L.	BOLDLY; REBELLIOUSLY
B - 13. OBSTINATE	M.	HOLY DAY
F - 14. HAUGHTILY	N.	AREA WHERE HOMES ARE LOCATED
H - 15. UNWAVERING	O.	DETAILED
J - 16. TROUSSEAU	P.	CULTURED; REFINED
M - 17. SABBATH	Q.	ANNOYED; IRRITATED
R - 18. SARCASTICALLY	R.	IN A CUTTING MANNER
N - 19. RESIDENTIAL	S.	NEEDLEWORK SIMILAR TO KNITTING
Q - 20. EXASPERATED	T.	VANDALIZE
L - 21. DEFIANTLY	U.	RECITED; SPOKE
X - 22. TRUDGED	V.	APPOINTED
A - 23. CONTEMPT	W.	SCORNFULLY
G - 24. SUBMERGED	X.	PLODDED; MARCHED
V - 25. DESIGNATED	Y.	CRIMINALS; HOOLIGANS

Number the Stars Vocabulary Matching 3

___ 1. IMPERIOUS
___ 2. DISDAINFULLY
___ 3. OBSTINATE
___ 4. SARCASTICALLY
___ 5. SABOTAGE
___ 6. SABBATH
___ 7. TROUSSEAU
___ 8. SOPHISTICATED
___ 9. INTONED
___ 10. INTRICATE
___ 11. SUBMERGED
___ 12. HOODLUMS
___ 13. EXASPERATED
___ 14. IMPASSIVE
___ 15. DUBIOUSLY
___ 16. DEFIANTLY
___ 17. SYNAGOGUE
___ 18. CROCHETING
___ 19. CONTEMPT
___ 20. UNWAVERING
___ 21. LANKY
___ 22. RABBI
___ 23. DESIGNATED
___ 24. TRUDGED
___ 25. RESIDENTIAL

A. PLODDED; MARCHED
B. JEWISH MINISTER
C. ITEMS BROUGHT TO MARRIAGE BY BRIDE
D. CULTURED; REFINED
E. JEWISH CHURCH
F. APPOINTED
G. RECITED; SPOKE
H. DETAILED
I. DOMINEERING; OVERBEARING
J. VANDALIZE
K. ANNOYED; IRRITATED
L. DISGUST; DISTASTE
M. AREA WHERE HOMES ARE LOCATED
N. IN A CUTTING MANNER
O. STABLE; STEADY
P. CRIMINALS; HOOLIGANS
Q. PLUNGED UNDERWATER
R. LEAN; THIN
S. HOLY DAY
T. NEEDLEWORK SIMILAR TO KNITTING
U. SCORNFULLY
V. DOUBTFULLY
W. UNEMOTIONAL; INDIFFERENT
X. BOLDLY; REBELLIOUSLY
Y. STUBBORN

Number the Stars Vocabulary Matching 3 Answer Key

I - 1. IMPERIOUS		A. PLODDED; MARCHED
U - 2. DISDAINFULLY		B. JEWISH MINISTER
Y - 3. OBSTINATE		C. ITEMS BROUGHT TO MARRIAGE BY BRIDE
N - 4. SARCASTICALLY		D. CULTURED; REFINED
J - 5. SABOTAGE		E. JEWISH CHURCH
S - 6. SABBATH		F. APPOINTED
C - 7. TROUSSEAU		G. RECITED; SPOKE
D - 8. SOPHISTICATED		H. DETAILED
G - 9. INTONED		I. DOMINEERING; OVERBEARING
H - 10. INTRICATE		J. VANDALIZE
Q - 11. SUBMERGED		K. ANNOYED; IRRITATED
P - 12. HOODLUMS		L. DISGUST; DISTASTE
K - 13. EXASPERATED		M. AREA WHERE HOMES ARE LOCATED
W - 14. IMPASSIVE		N. IN A CUTTING MANNER
V - 15. DUBIOUSLY		O. STABLE; STEADY
X - 16. DEFIANTLY		P. CRIMINALS; HOOLIGANS
E - 17. SYNAGOGUE		Q. PLUNGED UNDERWATER
T - 18. CROCHETING		R. LEAN; THIN
L - 19. CONTEMPT		S. HOLY DAY
O - 20. UNWAVERING		T. NEEDLEWORK SIMILAR TO KNITTING
R - 21. LANKY		U. SCORNFULLY
B - 22. RABBI		V. DOUBTFULLY
F - 23. DESIGNATED		W. UNEMOTIONAL; INDIFFERENT
A - 24. TRUDGED		X. BOLDLY; REBELLIOUSLY
M - 25. RESIDENTIAL		Y. STUBBORN

Number the Stars Vocabulary Matching 4

___ 1. BELLIGERENTLY   A. JEWISH CHURCH
___ 2. LANKY   B. PRESSED INTO
___ 3. IMPASSIVE   C. LEAN; THIN
___ 4. EXASPERATED   D. CRIMINALS; HOOLIGANS
___ 5. SABBATH   E. UNEMOTIONAL; INDIFFERENT
___ 6. DESIGNATED   F. STABLE; STEADY
___ 7. RESIDENTIAL   G. DISGUST; DISTASTE
___ 8. SYNAGOGUE   H. HOLY DAY
___ 9. DUBIOUSLY   I. APPOINTED
___10. CROCHETING   J. BOLDLY; REBELLIOUSLY
___11. DEFIANTLY   K. RECITED; SPOKE
___12. CONTEMPT   L. IN A HOSTILE MANNER
___13. TRUDGED   M. ARROGANTLY; HIGH AND MIGHTILY
___14. INTONED   N. AREA WHERE HOMES ARE LOCATED
___15. INTRICATE   O. DETAILED
___16. IMPERIOUS   P. DOUBTFULLY
___17. IMPRINTED   Q. STUBBORN
___18. SABOTAGE   R. JEWISH MINISTER
___19. OBSTINATE   S. VANDALIZE
___20. HOODLUMS   T. IN A CUTTING MANNER
___21. EMBROIDERED   U. DECORATED WITH NEEDLEWORK
___22. RABBI   V. ANNOYED; IRRITATED
___23. HAUGHTILY   W. DOMINEERING; OVERBEARING
___24. UNWAVERING   X. PLODDED; MARCHED
___25. SARCASTICALLY   Y. NEEDLEWORK SIMILAR TO KNITTING

Number the Stars Vocabulary Matching 4 Answer Key

L - 1. BELLIGERENTLY	A.	JEWISH CHURCH
C - 2. LANKY	B.	PRESSED INTO
E - 3. IMPASSIVE	C.	LEAN; THIN
V - 4. EXASPERATED	D.	CRIMINALS; HOOLIGANS
H - 5. SABBATH	E.	UNEMOTIONAL; INDIFFERENT
I - 6. DESIGNATED	F.	STABLE; STEADY
N - 7. RESIDENTIAL	G.	DISGUST; DISTASTE
A - 8. SYNAGOGUE	H.	HOLY DAY
P - 9. DUBIOUSLY	I.	APPOINTED
Y - 10. CROCHETING	J.	BOLDLY; REBELLIOUSLY
J - 11. DEFIANTLY	K.	RECITED; SPOKE
G - 12. CONTEMPT	L.	IN A HOSTILE MANNER
X - 13. TRUDGED	M.	ARROGANTLY; HIGH AND MIGHTILY
K - 14. INTONED	N.	AREA WHERE HOMES ARE LOCATED
O - 15. INTRICATE	O.	DETAILED
W - 16. IMPERIOUS	P.	DOUBTFULLY
B - 17. IMPRINTED	Q.	STUBBORN
S - 18. SABOTAGE	R.	JEWISH MINISTER
Q - 19. OBSTINATE	S.	VANDALIZE
D - 20. HOODLUMS	T.	IN A CUTTING MANNER
U - 21. EMBROIDERED	U.	DECORATED WITH NEEDLEWORK
R - 22. RABBI	V.	ANNOYED; IRRITATED
M - 23. HAUGHTILY	W.	DOMINEERING; OVERBEARING
F - 24. UNWAVERING	X.	PLODDED; MARCHED
T - 25. SARCASTICALLY	Y.	NEEDLEWORK SIMILAR TO KNITTING

Number the Stars Vocabulary Magic Squares 1

A. CONTEMPT
B. RABBI
C. HAUGHTILY
D. OBSTINATE
E. SABOTAGE
F. DEFIANTLY
G. EXASPERATED
H. IMPERIOUS
I. INTRICATE
J. SYNAGOGUE
K. LANKY
L. SOPHISTICATED
M. IMPRINTED
N. SABBATH
O. CROCHETING
P. TROUSSEAU

1. JEWISH MINISTER
2. ANNOYED; IRRITATED
3. LEAN; THIN
4. HOLY DAY
5. PRESSED INTO
6. CULTURED; REFINED
7. DOMINEERING; OVERBEARING
8. DISGUST; DISTASTE
9. ITEMS BROUGHT TO MARRIAGE BY BRIDE
10. DETAILED
11. VANDALIZE
12. STUBBORN
13. ARROGANTLY; HIGH AND MIGHTILY
14. BOLDLY; REBELLIOUSLY
15. JEWISH CHURCH
16. NEEDLEWORK SIMILAR TO KNITTING

A=	B=	C=	D=
E=	F=	G=	H=
I=	J=	K=	L=
M=	N=	O=	P=

Number the Stars Vocabulary Magic Squares 1 Answer Key

A. CONTEMPT
B. RABBI
C. HAUGHTILY
D. OBSTINATE
E. SABOTAGE
F. DEFIANTLY
G. EXASPERATED
H. IMPERIOUS
I. INTRICATE
J. SYNAGOGUE
K. LANKY
L. SOPHISTICATED
M. IMPRINTED
N. SABBATH
O. CROCHETING
P. TROUSSEAU

1. JEWISH MINISTER
2. ANNOYED; IRRITATED
3. LEAN; THIN
4. HOLY DAY
5. PRESSED INTO
6. CULTURED; REFINED
7. DOMINEERING; OVERBEARING
8. DISGUST; DISTASTE
9. ITEMS BROUGHT TO MARRIAGE BY BRIDE
10. DETAILED
11. VANDALIZE
12. STUBBORN
13. ARROGANTLY; HIGH AND MIGHTILY
14. BOLDLY; REBELLIOUSLY
15. JEWISH CHURCH
16. NEEDLEWORK SIMILAR TO KNITTING

A=8	B=1	C=13	D=12
E=11	F=14	G=2	H=7
I=10	J=15	K=3	L=6
M=5	N=4	O=16	P=9

Number the Stars Vocabulary Magic Squares 2

A. RESIDENTIAL
B. SABBATH
C. INTONED
D. BELLIGERENTLY
E. DISDAINFULLY
F. INTRICATE
G. TRUDGED
H. IMPASSIVE
I. HAUGHTILY
J. DEFIANTLY
K. SARCASTICALLY
L. SOPHISTICATED
M. RABBI
N. UNWAVERING
O. SYNAGOGUE
P. SABOTAGE

1. UNEMOTIONAL; INDIFFERENT
2. JEWISH MINISTER
3. HOLY DAY
4. IN A CUTTING MANNER
5. BOLDLY; REBELLIOUSLY
6. RECITED; SPOKE
7. VANDALIZE
8. SCORNFULLY
9. JEWISH CHURCH
10. DETAILED
11. ARROGANTLY; HIGH AND MIGHTILY
12. IN A HOSTILE MANNER
13. AREA WHERE HOMES ARE LOCATED
14. CULTURED; REFINED
15. PLODDED; MARCHED
16. STABLE; STEADY

A=	B=	C=	D=
E=	F=	G=	H=
I=	J=	K=	L=
M=	N=	O=	P=

Number the Stars Vocabulary Magic Squares 2 Answer Key

A. RESIDENTIAL
B. SABBATH
C. INTONED
D. BELLIGERENTLY
E. DISDAINFULLY
F. INTRICATE
G. TRUDGED
H. IMPASSIVE
I. HAUGHTILY
J. DEFIANTLY
K. SARCASTICALLY
L. SOPHISTICATED
M. RABBI
N. UNWAVERING
O. SYNAGOGUE
P. SABOTAGE

1. UNEMOTIONAL; INDIFFERENT
2. JEWISH MINISTER
3. HOLY DAY
4. IN A CUTTING MANNER
5. BOLDLY; REBELLIOUSLY
6. RECITED; SPOKE
7. VANDALIZE
8. SCORNFULLY
9. JEWISH CHURCH
10. DETAILED
11. ARROGANTLY; HIGH AND MIGHTILY
12. IN A HOSTILE MANNER
13. AREA WHERE HOMES ARE LOCATED
14. CULTURED; REFINED
15. PLODDED; MARCHED
16. STABLE; STEADY

A=13	B=3	C=6	D=12
E=8	F=10	G=15	H=1
I=11	J=5	K=4	L=14
M=2	N=16	O=9	P=7

Number the Stars Vocabulary Magic Squares 3

A. INTONED
B. CONTEMPT
C. RESIDENTIAL
D. RABBI
E. SABOTAGE
F. TRUDGED
G. IMPRINTED
H. BELLIGERENTLY
I. SARCASTICALLY
J. EXASPERATED
K. EMBROIDERED
L. TROUSSEAU
M. LANKY
N. SOPHISTICATED
O. OBSTINATE
P. INTRICATE

1. AREA WHERE HOMES ARE LOCATED
2. ANNOYED; IRRITATED
3. PLODDED; MARCHED
4. STUBBORN
5. DETAILED
6. VANDALIZE
7. IN A CUTTING MANNER
8. JEWISH MINISTER
9. LEAN; THIN
10. IN A HOSTILE MANNER
11. ITEMS BROUGHT TO MARRIAGE BY BRIDE
12. RECITED; SPOKE
13. DISGUST; DISTASTE
14. DECORATED WITH NEEDLEWORK
15. PRESSED INTO
16. CULTURED; REFINED

A=	B=	C=	D=
E=	F=	G=	H=
I=	J=	K=	L=
M=	N=	O=	P=

Number the Stars Vocabulary Magic Squares 3 Answer Key

A. INTONED
B. CONTEMPT
C. RESIDENTIAL
D. RABBI
E. SABOTAGE
F. TRUDGED
G. IMPRINTED
H. BELLIGERENTLY
I. SARCASTICALLY
J. EXASPERATED
K. EMBROIDERED
L. TROUSSEAU
M. LANKY
N. SOPHISTICATED
O. OBSTINATE
P. INTRICATE

1. AREA WHERE HOMES ARE LOCATED
2. ANNOYED; IRRITATED
3. PLODDED; MARCHED
4. STUBBORN
5. DETAILED
6. VANDALIZE
7. IN A CUTTING MANNER
8. JEWISH MINISTER
9. LEAN; THIN
10. IN A HOSTILE MANNER
11. ITEMS BROUGHT TO MARRIAGE BY BRIDE
12. RECITED; SPOKE
13. DISGUST; DISTASTE
14. DECORATED WITH NEEDLEWORK
15. PRESSED INTO
16. CULTURED; REFINED

A=12	B=13	C=1	D=8
E=6	F=3	G=15	H=10
I=7	J=2	K=14	L=11
M=9	N=16	O=4	P=5

Number the Stars Vocabulary Magic Squares 4

A. TROUSSEAU
B. INTONED
C. HOODLUMS
D. UNWAVERING
E. SABOTAGE
F. OBSTINATE
G. SARCASTICALLY
H. DESIGNATED
I. EMBROIDERED
J. RABBI
K. DEFIANTLY
L. DUBIOUSLY
M. HAUGHTILY
N. RESIDENTIAL
O. IMPRINTED
P. CONTEMPT

1. APPOINTED
2. ITEMS BROUGHT TO MARRIAGE BY BRIDE
3. RECITED; SPOKE
4. IN A CUTTING MANNER
5. JEWISH MINISTER
6. PRESSED INTO
7. DISGUST; DISTASTE
8. DECORATED WITH NEEDLEWORK
9. BOLDLY; REBELLIOUSLY
10. AREA WHERE HOMES ARE LOCATED
11. ARROGANTLY; HIGH AND MIGHTILY
12. DOUBTFULLY
13. VANDALIZE
14. STABLE; STEADY
15. CRIMINALS; HOOLIGANS
16. STUBBORN

A=	B=	C=	D=
E=	F=	G=	H=
I=	J=	K=	L=
M=	N=	O=	P=

Number the Stars Vocabulary Magic Squares 4 Answer Key

A. TROUSSEAU
B. INTONED
C. HOODLUMS
D. UNWAVERING
E. SABOTAGE
F. OBSTINATE
G. SARCASTICALLY
H. DESIGNATED
I. EMBROIDERED
J. RABBI
K. DEFIANTLY
L. DUBIOUSLY
M. HAUGHTILY
N. RESIDENTIAL
O. IMPRINTED
P. CONTEMPT

1. APPOINTED
2. ITEMS BROUGHT TO MARRIAGE BY BRIDE
3. RECITED; SPOKE
4. IN A CUTTING MANNER
5. JEWISH MINISTER
6. PRESSED INTO
7. DISGUST; DISTASTE
8. DECORATED WITH NEEDLEWORK
9. BOLDLY; REBELLIOUSLY
10. AREA WHERE HOMES ARE LOCATED
11. ARROGANTLY; HIGH AND MIGHTILY
12. DOUBTFULLY
13. VANDALIZE
14. STABLE; STEADY
15. CRIMINALS; HOOLIGANS
16. STUBBORN

A=2	B=3	C=15	D=14
E=13	F=16	G=4	H=1
I=8	J=5	K=9	L=12
M=11	N=10	O=6	P=7

Number the Stars Vocabulary Word Search 1

```
H Z Y G M Z M X D T C Z S S L B C G I R
X A G P D R Y W Z T H B Y U G T Z D M H
K L U S H D I Q P H E C N B N D Z E P H
Z G H G B V M N H T N H A M I K S F A L
L T H M H X P T A Y Z R G E T V Q I S L
S H Y N H T R C L N E M O R E W W A S Y
Y L L U F N I A D S I D G G H M S N I S
S F L F V R N L I Q A N U E C U M T V B
A B A H T K T D Y T I B E D O L U L E Y
B F C N Y Q E F D R R T B I R B L Y B X
O N I T Y N D H E U N O R A C J D Y E D
T G T N T K Y V R T B E U U T V O R L P
A P S I B B A R E P P I J S D H O F L L
G T A T J W Y L D M V W O M S G H C I R
E L C F N B P D I E Y H I U D E E F G J
J N R U H H W C O T F H N E S M A D E K
C S A F H F D G R N C F T O Q L B U R K
X G S K G X K W B O T A O B Y Z Y M E R
X K P Z N Q X L M C R X N S Z Q T D N P
Z Z S M C Y X R E E S K E T V Y J X T D
K R J R K L S X P B Z R D I W X V L L K
D E T A C I T S I H P O S N Q H Q N Y V
C S G Q Y F A Q X M X L G A X Y F V D X
Z K P Z J X D E S I G N A T E D H G N B
V W D W E T W F R L H H C E Q V P R L H
```

ANNOYED; IRRITATED (11)
APPOINTED (10)
AREA WHERE HOMES ARE LOCATED (11)
ARROGANTLY; HIGH AND MIGHTILY (9)
BOLDLY; REBELLIOUSLY (9)
CRIMINALS; HOOLIGANS (8)
CULTURED; REFINED (13)
DECORATED WITH NEEDLEWORK (11)
DETAILED (9)
DISGUST; DISTASTE (8)
DOMINEERING; OVERBEARING (9)
DOUBTFULLY (9)
HOLY DAY (7)
IN A CUTTING MANNER (13)
IN A HOSTILE MANNER (13)
ITEMS BROUGHT TO MARRIAGE BY
 BRIDE (9)
JEWISH CHURCH (9)
JEWISH MINISTER (5)
LEAN; THIN (5)
NEEDLEWORK SIMILAR TO KNITTING (10)
PLODDED; MARCHED (7)
PLUNGED UNDERWATER (9)

PRESSED INTO (9)
RECITED; SPOKE (7)
SCORNFULLY (12)
STABLE; STEADY (10)
STUBBORN (9)
UNEMOTIONAL; INDIFFERENT (9)
VANDALIZE (8)

Number the Stars Vocabulary Word Search 1 Answer Key

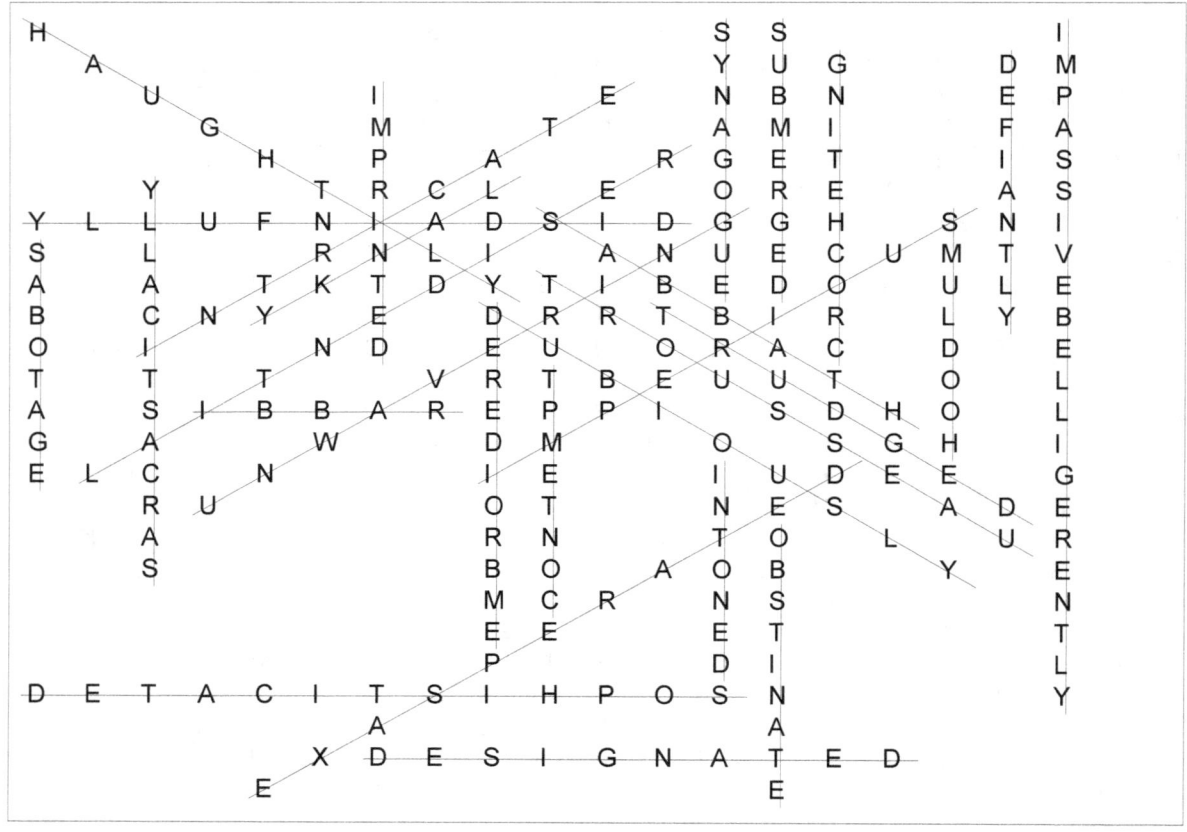

ANNOYED; IRRITATED (11)
APPOINTED (10)
AREA WHERE HOMES ARE LOCATED (11)
ARROGANTLY; HIGH AND MIGHTILY (9)
BOLDLY; REBELLIOUSLY (9)
CRIMINALS; HOOLIGANS (8)
CULTURED; REFINED (13)
DECORATED WITH NEEDLEWORK (11)
DETAILED (9)
DISGUST; DISTASTE (8)
DOMINEERING; OVERBEARING (9)
DOUBTFULLY (9)
HOLY DAY (7)
IN A CUTTING MANNER (13)
IN A HOSTILE MANNER (13)
ITEMS BROUGHT TO MARRIAGE BY
  BRIDE (9)
JEWISH CHURCH (9)
JEWISH MINISTER (5)
LEAN; THIN (5)
NEEDLEWORK SIMILAR TO KNITTING (10)
PLODDED; MARCHED (7)
PLUNGED UNDERWATER (9)

PRESSED INTO (9)
RECITED; SPOKE (7)
SCORNFULLY (12)
STABLE; STEADY (10)
STUBBORN (9)
UNEMOTIONAL; INDIFFERENT (9)
VANDALIZE (8)

Number the Stars Vocabulary Word Search 2

```
T D U B I O U S L Y L T N A I F E D D N
O R D E S I G N A T E D V P R T E E C S
B N O T R I T M C B F G V B N L T G A R
S M M U B F Y J N H O G N P J A A R T S
T D J B S B V V T T B T G H R H C E H X
I S A U M S Q N D N T C A E M A I M M F
N R I N U E E B C R Y N P G S W R B K H
A S M W L M K A G H S S H T E J T U B W
T S P A D B B Z U F A D I Y N P N S E S
E H A V O R D B T X X C L Y T X I M L J
T N S E O O T W E G A L Q P P W R G L G
X T S R H I N S P L U V G G B R Z F I K
D N I I K D V C L F L B F L H V P M G C
S J V N G E L Y N R G V K X X Q P Z E Y
H S E G L R Z I C E Q G B L M E Z G R K
G A Y J L E A T O S N Z J L R V D D E C
T B U S N D E T N I R P M I M F K E N G
L B X G S D X Q T D B I O K W M U G T K
K A F I H D T E E E F U N L P G M D L D
R T D D T T H L M N S Y Y T O W H U Y F
V H M Q K C I R P T V K B G O M H R G P
P R N T O X G L T I N R A R Y N B T K D
N G F R J X F W Y A Y N P C Y S E M S D
M S C N J X K C L L Y V P G K M D D P H
V R D E T A C I T S I H P O S F B W L F
```

ANNOYED; IRRITATED (11)
APPOINTED (10)
AREA WHERE HOMES ARE LOCATED (11)
ARROGANTLY; HIGH AND MIGHTILY (9)
BOLDLY; REBELLIOUSLY (9)
CRIMINALS; HOOLIGANS (8)
CULTURED; REFINED (13)
DECORATED WITH NEEDLEWORK (11)
DETAILED (9)
DISGUST; DISTASTE (8)
DOMINEERING; OVERBEARING (9)
DOUBTFULLY (9)
HOLY DAY (7)
IN A CUTTING MANNER (13)
IN A HOSTILE MANNER (13)
ITEMS BROUGHT TO MARRIAGE BY BRIDE (9)
JEWISH CHURCH (9)
JEWISH MINISTER (5)
LEAN; THIN (5)
NEEDLEWORK SIMILAR TO KNITTING (10)
PLODDED; MARCHED (7)
PLUNGED UNDERWATER (9)

PRESSED INTO (9)
RECITED; SPOKE (7)
SCORNFULLY (12)
STABLE; STEADY (10)
STUBBORN (9)
UNEMOTIONAL; INDIFFERENT (9)
VANDALIZE (8)

Number the Stars Vocabulary Word Search 2 Answer Key

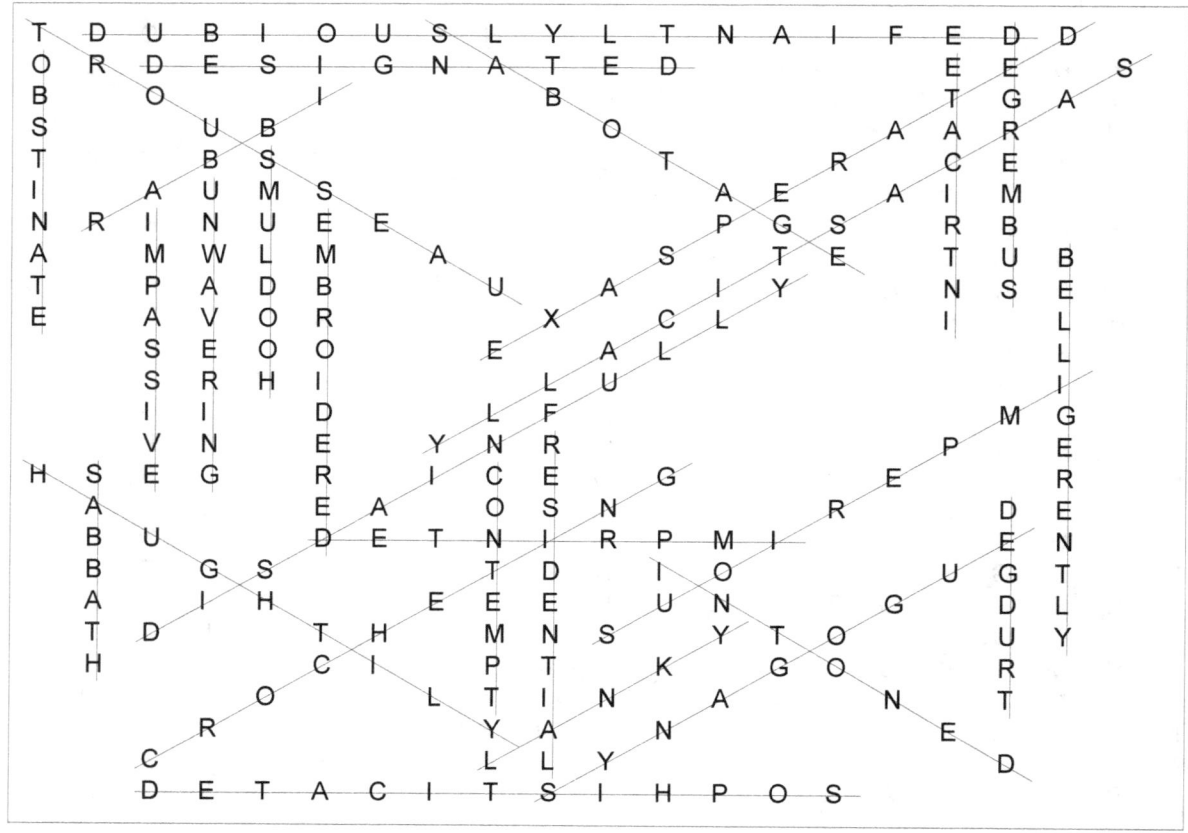

ANNOYED; IRRITATED (11)
APPOINTED (10)
AREA WHERE HOMES ARE LOCATED (11)
ARROGANTLY; HIGH AND MIGHTILY (9)
BOLDLY; REBELLIOUSLY (9)
CRIMINALS; HOOLIGANS (8)
CULTURED; REFINED (13)
DECORATED WITH NEEDLEWORK (11)
DETAILED (9)
DISGUST; DISTASTE (8)
DOMINEERING; OVERBEARING (9)
DOUBTFULLY (9)
HOLY DAY (7)
IN A CUTTING MANNER (13)
IN A HOSTILE MANNER (13)
ITEMS BROUGHT TO MARRIAGE BY
  BRIDE (9)
JEWISH CHURCH (9)
JEWISH MINISTER (5)
LEAN; THIN (5)
NEEDLEWORK SIMILAR TO KNITTING (10)
PLODDED; MARCHED (7)
PLUNGED UNDERWATER (9)

PRESSED INTO (9)
RECITED; SPOKE (7)
SCORNFULLY (12)
STABLE; STEADY (10)
STUBBORN (9)
UNEMOTIONAL; INDIFFERENT (9)
VANDALIZE (8)

Number the Stars Vocabulary Word Search 3

```
T R O U S S E A U R E S I D E N T I A L
F T R S J D J H D Z B J J Y Y Z C R M L
M P K G Z B D E T A C I T S I H P O S X
S U B M E R G E D E T A R E P S A X E J
H Y Y S Q D V G V H Y R Z G H N M Z D N
J V F C U F W W W G J K L M Y I P T E X
V J R R G N T Q H P Q H P F R M T V R M
H D T J L D H X D O Z M V T X P S Y E H
N F V N V E L H F G O B R H Y E T P D R
T O K Q F N G P R R D D J Q V R D H I W
L C B Z D O T Y D T A R L C K I E W O G
S W S S W T S U X H W B H U F O F D R Y
C A H M T N B S I W J J B F M U I B B C
F H B N H I F L S M G E V I S S A P M I
H Y A O O X N Y B B P N G C D B N U E S
P S S U T S N A B Y J R N A V X T N T Q
B R S K G A D E T A N G I S E D L W A W
X L K M G H G P T E C N T N T G Y A C V
Y L M O G T T E K H F K E P T N H V I Q
D Q G M V Y C I T U N W H W M E B E R C
D U Z B K K X A L L K H C W K Q D R T C
E Q H N M W B L L Y V D O C B P S I N B
H D A B B B Y N M R Y R R H C J J N I D
T L L F A T P M E T N O C G H R H G C M
R Q T S B E L L I G E R E N T L Y D P F
```

BELLIGERENTLY	EMBROIDERED	INTONED	SABOTAGE
CONTEMPT	EXASPERATED	INTRICATE	SOPHISTICATED
CROCHETING	HAUGHTILY	LANKY	SUBMERGED
DEFIANTLY	HOODLUMS	OBSTINATE	SYNAGOGUE
DESIGNATED	IMPASSIVE	RABBI	TROUSSEAU
DISDAINFULLY	IMPERIOUS	RESIDENTIAL	TRUDGED
DUBIOUSLY	IMPRINTED	SABBATH	UNWAVERING

Number the Stars Vocabulary Word Search 3 Answer Key

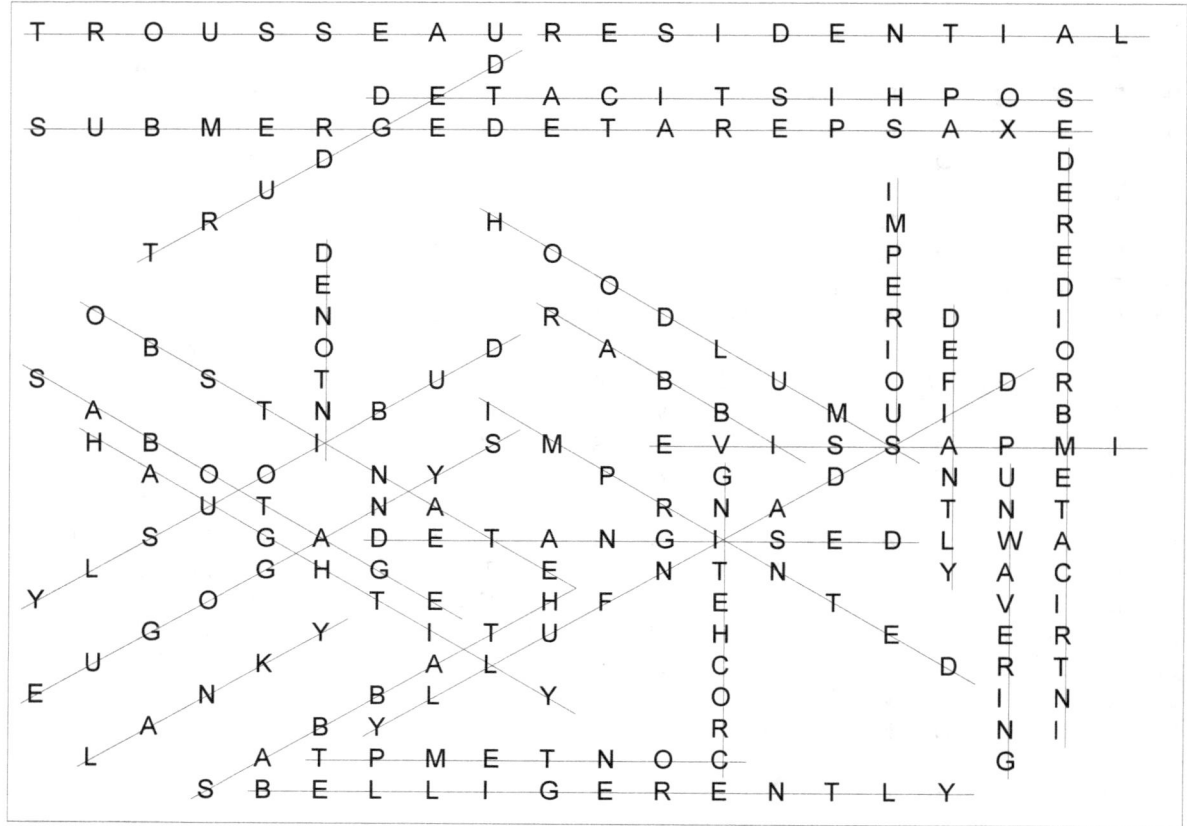

BELLIGERENTLY	EMBROIDERED	INTONED	SABOTAGE
CONTEMPT	EXASPERATED	INTRICATE	SOPHISTICATED
CROCHETING	HAUGHTILY	LANKY	SUBMERGED
DEFIANTLY	HOODLUMS	OBSTINATE	SYNAGOGUE
DESIGNATED	IMPASSIVE	RABBI	TROUSSEAU
DISDAINFULLY	IMPERIOUS	RESIDENTIAL	TRUDGED
DUBIOUSLY	IMPRINTED	SABBATH	UNWAVERING

Number the Stars Vocabulary Word Search 4

```
B E L L I G E R E N T L Y C W S F D B R
R G R S F C M W N H L N R L P U Y Z N D
C H K C G J L W H M F B Z B R B W W E N
M K Q K B D D E R E D I O R B M E T L X
B B W V Y G W C M R J H B Y J E A C Y F
C S K H S D R L R B F J Z H L R C T N S
Y O A G H W M C D O Y S Q B E G V Y U R
W F N R R G B H E G C C V P J E Z O Q M
R L C T C S L P N Z S H S L X D I C L L
J Y J T E A F C O X Q A E F R W Y S S
H F B Y J M S J T S X G Z T E S D Y A N
T G D L W W P T N E S J A P I Y K B B H
R E S I D E N T I A L C M D X N B D O W
U Q O T S P C B J C I I E K A A G U T Z
D V B H H D B S H T A F M L T G I B A M
G N S G K A A D S O I L J H R O M I G J
E T T U R H W I E A O L L T S G P O E X
D N I A P X H T N S C D R Y Q U R U T V
Y H N H R P A T K F I O L T Q E I S S W
R X A L O C L T Z J U G Z U S P N L V J
M Q T S I Y F H T S V L N H M L T Y D H
P Y E R X B H M S Z D H L A F S E M N R
L L T J X F K E H C C W H Y T H D F H Z
G N I R E V A W N U P H W V V E W T Z N
I J P Y H U J I M P A S S I V E D L M F
```

BELLIGERENTLY	EXASPERATED	LANKY	SUBMERGED
CONTEMPT	HAUGHTILY	OBSTINATE	SYNAGOGUE
CROCHETING	HOODLUMS	RABBI	TROUSSEAU
DEFIANTLY	IMPASSIVE	RESIDENTIAL	TRUDGED
DESIGNATED	IMPERIOUS	SABBATH	UNWAVERING
DISDAINFULLY	IMPRINTED	SABOTAGE	
DUBIOUSLY	INTONED	SARCASTICALLY	
EMBROIDERED	INTRICATE	SOPHISTICATED	

Number the Stars Vocabulary Word Search 4 Answer Key

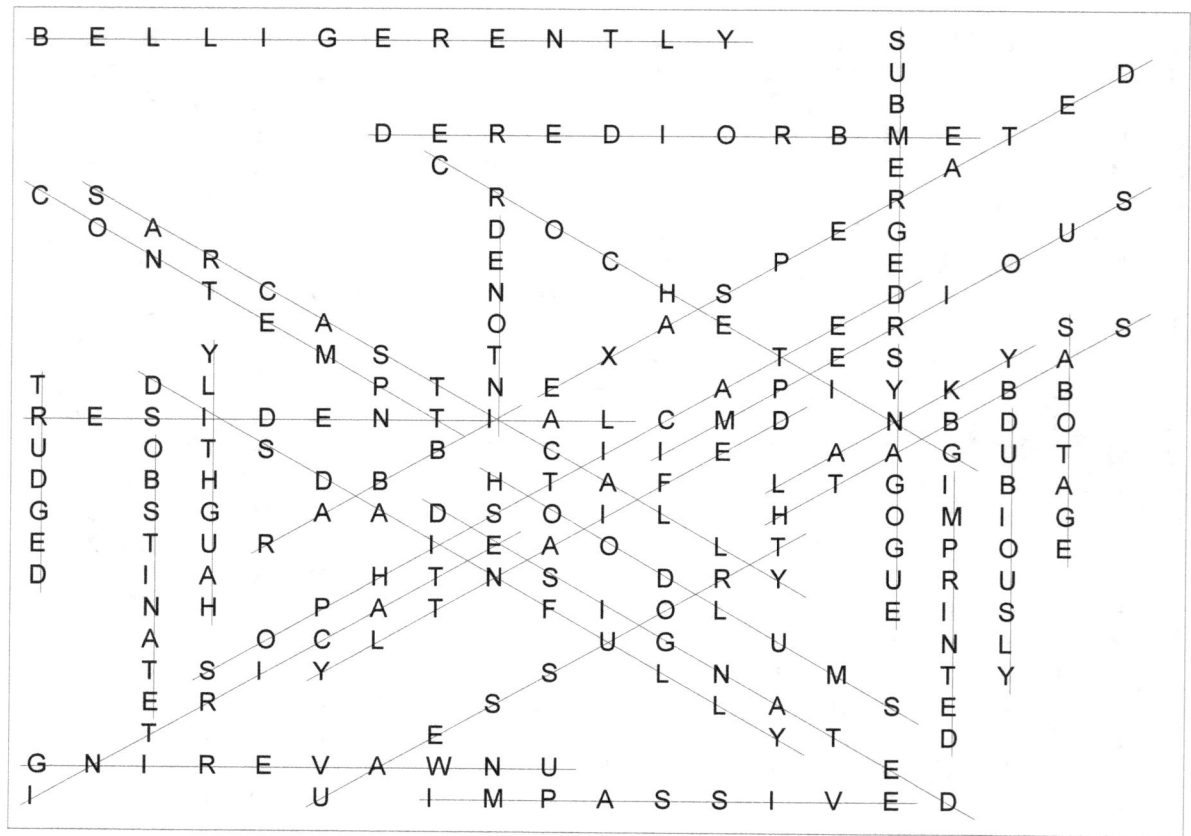

BELLIGERENTLY	EXASPERATED	LANKY	SUBMERGED
CONTEMPT	HAUGHTILY	OBSTINATE	SYNAGOGUE
CROCHETING	HOODLUMS	RABBI	TROUSSEAU
DEFIANTLY	IMPASSIVE	RESIDENTIAL	TRUDGED
DESIGNATED	IMPERIOUS	SABBATH	UNWAVERING
DISDAINFULLY	IMPRINTED	SABOTAGE	
DUBIOUSLY	INTONED	SARCASTICALLY	
EMBROIDERED	INTRICATE	SOPHISTICATED	

Number the Stars Vocabulary Crossword 1

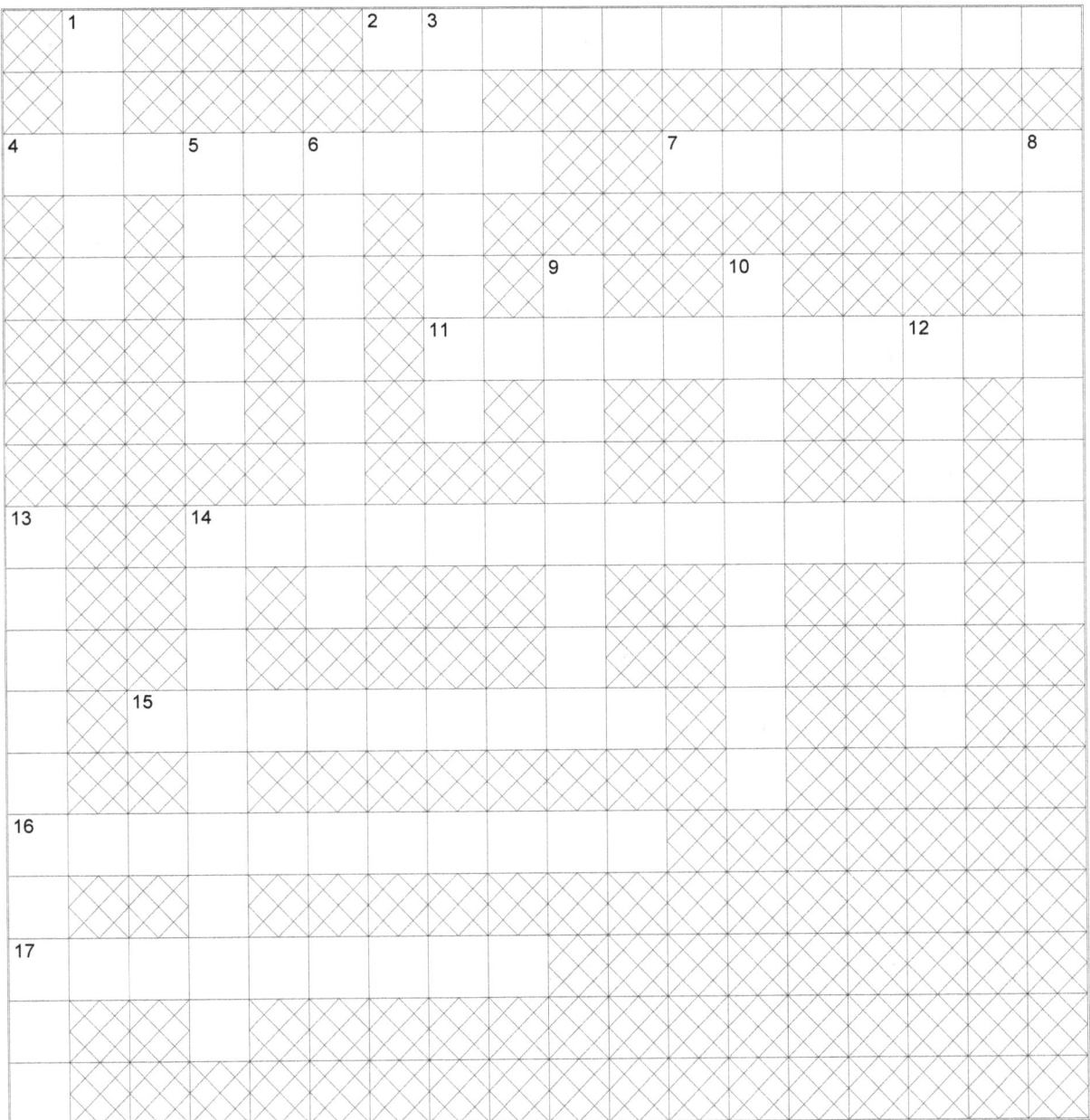

Across
2. SCORNFULLY
4. DETAILED
7. HOLY DAY
11. ANNOYED; IRRITATED
14. CULTURED; REFINED
15. PRESSED INTO
16. DECORATED WITH NEEDLEWORK
17. DOMINEERING; OVERBEARING

Down
1. LEAN; THIN
3. RECITED; SPOKE
5. JEWISH MINISTER
6. DISGUST; DISTASTE
8. CRIMINALS; HOOLIGANS
9. VANDALIZE
10. BOLDLY; REBELLIOUSLY
12. PLODDED; MARCHED
13. STABLE; STEADY
14. PLUNGED UNDERWATER

Number the Stars Vocabulary Crossword 1 Answer Key

	1 L		2 D	3 I	S	D	A	I	N	F	U	L	L	Y
	A			N										
4 I	N	5 T	6 R	I	C	A	T	E		7 S	A	B	B	A	T	8 H
	K		A		O		O									O
	Y		B		N		N		9 S		10 D					O
			B		T		11 E	X	A	S	P	E	R	A	12 T	E	D
			I		E		D		B		F				R		L
					M				O		I				U		U
13 U		14 S	O	P	H	I	S	T	I	C	A	T	E	D		M
N		U		T				A			N				G		S
W		B						G			T				E	
A		15 I	M	P	R	I	N	T	E	D		L			D	
V		E										Y				
16 E	M	B	R	O	I	D	E	R	E	D						
R		G														
17 I	M	P	E	R	I	O	U	S								
N		D														
G																

Across
- 2. SCORNFULLY
- 4. DETAILED
- 7. HOLY DAY
- 11. ANNOYED; IRRITATED
- 14. CULTURED; REFINED
- 15. PRESSED INTO
- 16. DECORATED WITH NEEDLEWORK
- 17. DOMINEERING; OVERBEARING

Down
- 1. LEAN; THIN
- 3. RECITED; SPOKE
- 5. JEWISH MINISTER
- 6. DISGUST; DISTASTE
- 8. CRIMINALS; HOOLIGANS
- 9. VANDALIZE
- 10. BOLDLY; REBELLIOUSLY
- 12. PLODDED; MARCHED
- 13. STABLE; STEADY
- 14. PLUNGED UNDERWATER

Number the Stars Vocabulary Crossword 2

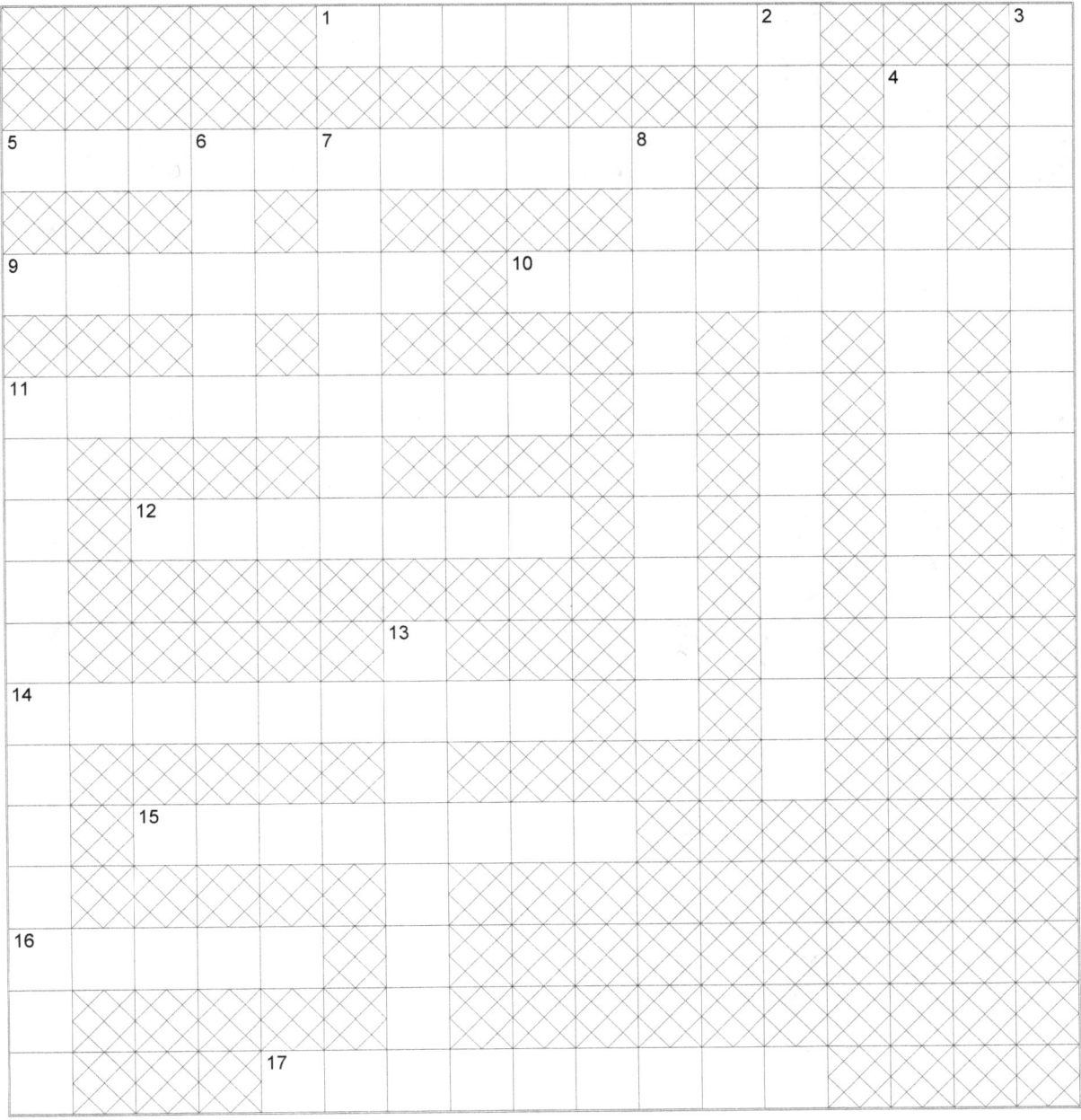

Across
1. CRIMINALS; HOOLIGANS
5. DECORATED WITH NEEDLEWORK
9. HOLY DAY
10. STUBBORN
11. BOLDLY; REBELLIOUSLY
12. PLODDED; MARCHED
14. DOMINEERING; OVERBEARING
15. VANDALIZE
16. LEAN; THIN
17. DETAILED

Down
2. CULTURED; REFINED
3. PLUNGED UNDERWATER
4. STABLE; STEADY
6. JEWISH MINISTER
7. RECITED; SPOKE
8. APPOINTED
11. SCORNFULLY
13. DISGUST; DISTASTE

Number the Stars Vocabulary Crossword 2 Answer Key

					¹H	O	O	D	L	U	M	S			³S
											²S		⁴U		U
⁵E	M	⁶B	R	O	⁷I	D	E	R	⁸E	D		P		N	B
			A		N				E			H		W	M
⁹S	A	B	B	A	T	H		¹⁰O	B	S	T	I	N	A	T	E
			B		O				I			S		V	R
¹¹D	E	F	I	A	N	T	L	Y		G		T		E	G
I					E					N		I		R	E
S		¹²T	R	U	D	G	E	D		A		C		I	D
D										T		A		N	
A						¹³C				E		T		G	
¹⁴I	M	P	E	R	I	O	U	S		D		E			
N						N						D			
F		¹⁵S	A	B	O	T	A	G	E						
U						E									
¹⁶L	A	N	K	Y		M									
L						P									
Y				¹⁷I	N	T	R	I	C	A	T	E			

Across
1. CRIMINALS; HOOLIGANS
5. DECORATED WITH NEEDLEWORK
9. HOLY DAY
10. STUBBORN
11. BOLDLY; REBELLIOUSLY
12. PLODDED; MARCHED
14. DOMINEERING; OVERBEARING
15. VANDALIZE
16. LEAN; THIN
17. DETAILED

Down
2. CULTURED; REFINED
3. PLUNGED UNDERWATER
4. STABLE; STEADY
6. JEWISH MINISTER
7. RECITED; SPOKE
8. APPOINTED
11. SCORNFULLY
13. DISGUST; DISTASTE

Number the Stars Vocabulary Crossword 3

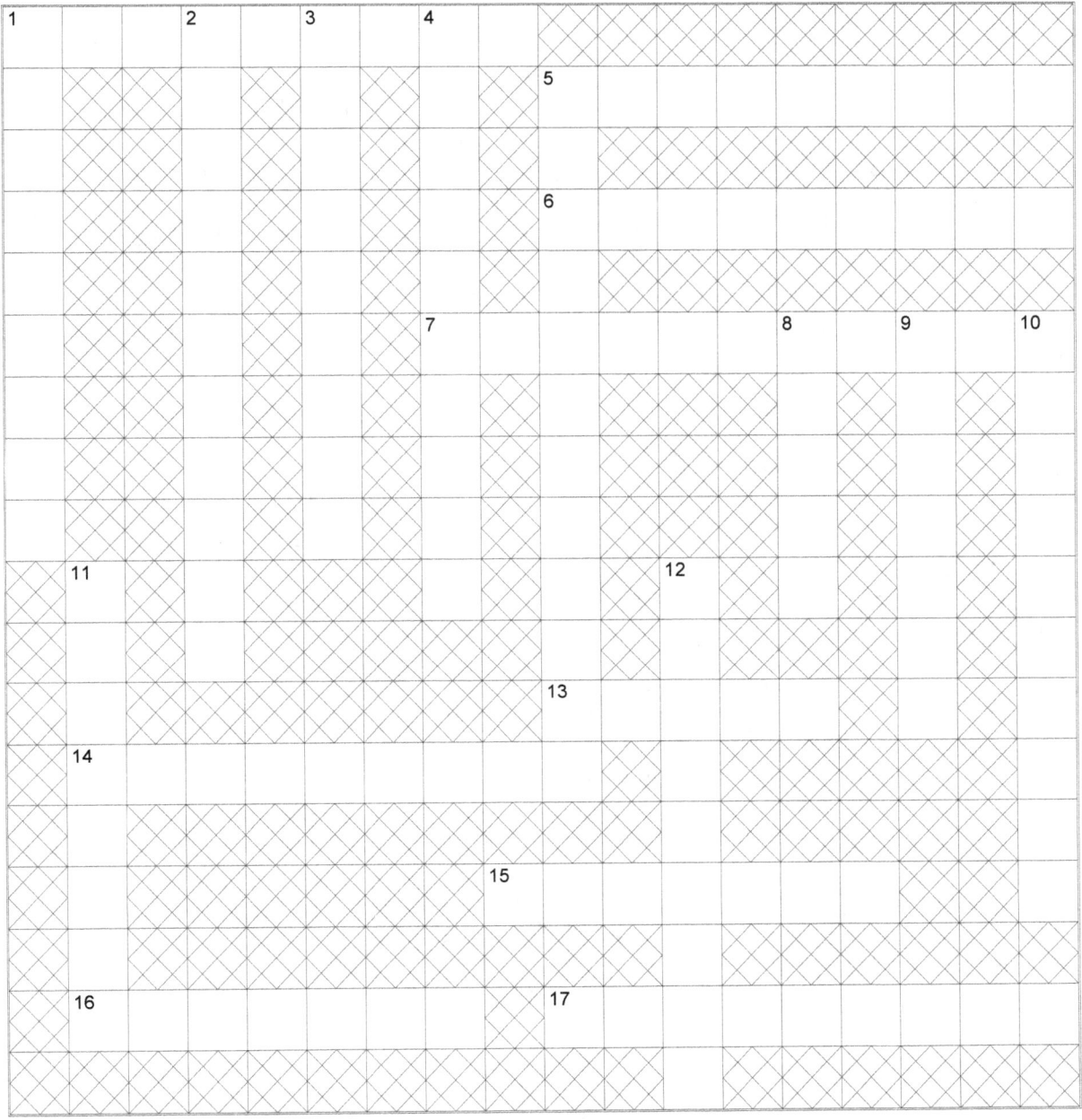

Across
1. DOMINEERING; OVERBEARING
5. BOLDLY; REBELLIOUSLY
6. PLUNGED UNDERWATER
7. ANNOYED; IRRITATED
13. LEAN; THIN
14. DOUBTFULLY
15. RECITED; SPOKE
16. HOLY DAY
17. ARROGANTLY; HIGH AND MIGHTILY

Down
1. DETAILED
2. DECORATED WITH NEEDLEWORK
3. PRESSED INTO
4. STABLE; STEADY
5. SCORNFULLY
8. JEWISH MINISTER
9. PLODDED; MARCHED
10. APPOINTED
11. CRIMINALS; HOOLIGANS
12. JEWISH CHURCH

Number the Stars Vocabulary Crossword 3 Answer Key

	1 I	M	2 P	E	3 R	I	4 O	U	S						
	N		M		M		N		5 D	E	F	I	A	N	T	L	Y
	T		B		P		W		I						
	R		R		R		A		6 S	U	B	M	E	R	G	E	D
	I		O		I		V		D						
	C		I		N		7 E	X	A	S	P	8 E	R	9 A	T	10 E	D
	A		D		T		R		I			A		R		E
	T		E		E		I		N			B		U		S
	E		R		D		N		F			B		D		I
		11 H	E				G		U		12 S		I		G		G
		O		D					L		Y				E		N
		O					13 L	A	N	K	Y				D		A
		14 D	U	B	I	O	U	S	L	Y			A				T
		L									G					E
		U					15 I	N	T	O	N	E	D			D
		M									G				
		16 S	A	B	B	A	T	H		17 H	A	U	G	H	T	I	L	Y
										E					

Across
1. DOMINEERING; OVERBEARING
5. BOLDLY; REBELLIOUSLY
6. PLUNGED UNDERWATER
7. ANNOYED; IRRITATED
13. LEAN; THIN
14. DOUBTFULLY
15. RECITED; SPOKE
16. HOLY DAY
17. ARROGANTLY; HIGH AND MIGHTILY

3. PRESSED INTO
4. STABLE; STEADY
5. SCORNFULLY
8. JEWISH MINISTER
9. PLODDED; MARCHED
10. APPOINTED
11. CRIMINALS; HOOLIGANS
12. JEWISH CHURCH

Down
1. DETAILED
2. DECORATED WITH NEEDLEWORK

Number the Stars Vocabulary Crossword 4

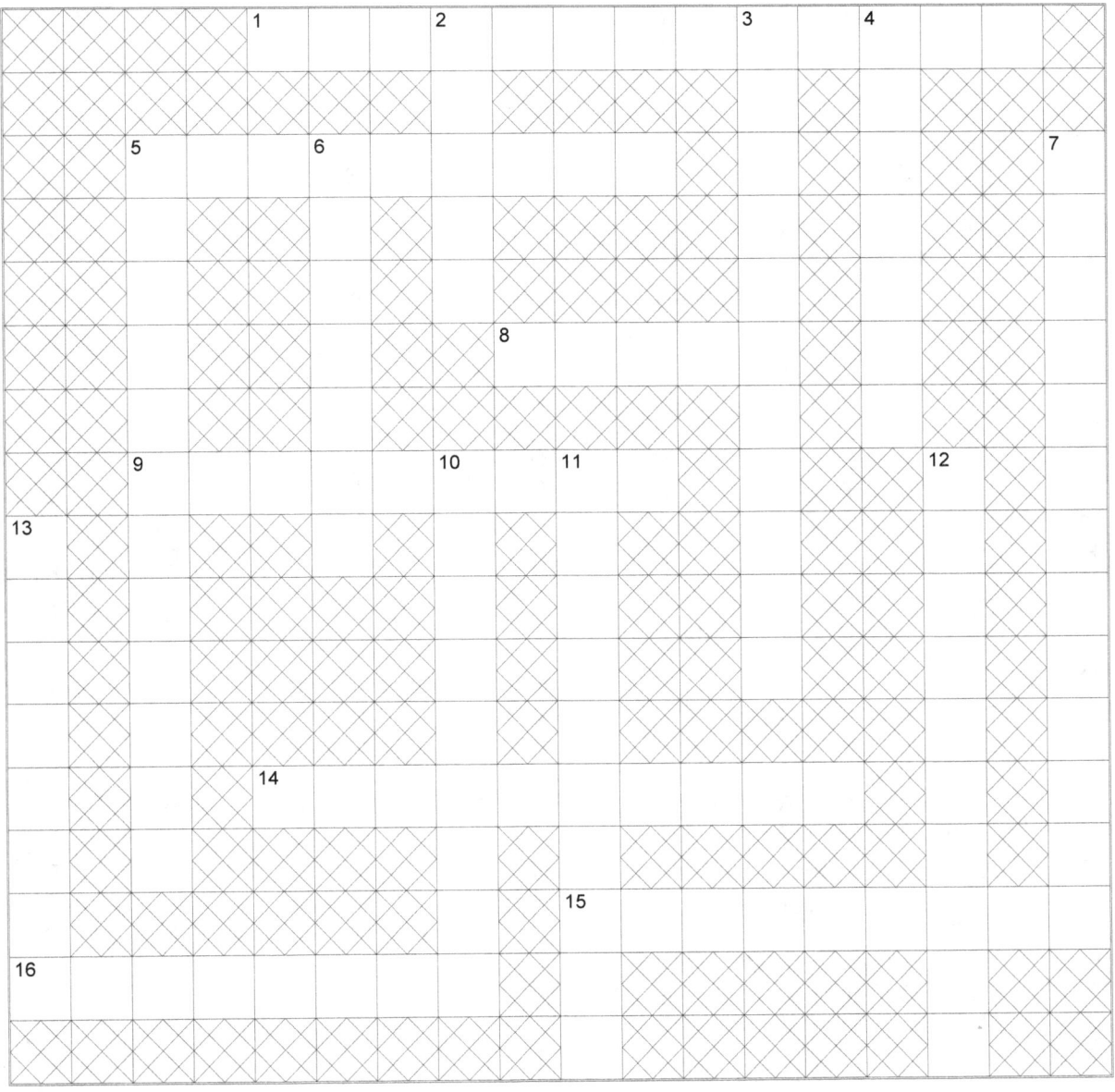

Across
1. IN A HOSTILE MANNER
5. BOLDLY; REBELLIOUSLY
8. JEWISH MINISTER
9. DOMINEERING; OVERBEARING
14. NEEDLEWORK SIMILAR TO KNITTING
15. PRESSED INTO
16. VANDALIZE

Down
2. LEAN; THIN
3. DECORATED WITH NEEDLEWORK
4. PLODDED; MARCHED
5. SCORNFULLY
6. RECITED; SPOKE
7. CULTURED; REFINED
10. DETAILED
11. STABLE; STEADY
12. APPOINTED
13. CRIMINALS; HOOLIGANS

Number the Stars Vocabulary Crossword 4 Answer Key

Across
1. IN A HOSTILE MANNER
5. BOLDLY; REBELLIOUSLY
8. JEWISH MINISTER
9. DOMINEERING; OVERBEARING
14. NEEDLEWORK SIMILAR TO KNITTING
15. PRESSED INTO
16. VANDALIZE

Down
2. LEAN; THIN
3. DECORATED WITH NEEDLEWORK
4. PLODDED; MARCHED
5. SCORNFULLY
6. RECITED; SPOKE
7. CULTURED; REFINED
10. DETAILED
11. STABLE; STEADY
12. APPOINTED
13. CRIMINALS; HOOLIGANS

Number the Stars Vocabulary Juggle Letters 1

1. KANLY = 1. _____
   LEAN; THIN

2. UUIOYSBDL = 2. _____
   DOUBTFULLY

3. DRIDBEEOMER = 3. _____
   DECORATED WITH NEEDLEWORK

4. ESDLRNTEAII = 4. _____
   AREA WHERE HOMES ARE LOCATED

5. DESMERBUG = 5. _____
   PLUNGED UNDERWATER

6. HITEPADSCSITO = 6. _____
   CULTURED; REFINED

7. OUEURASST = 7. _____
   ITEMS BROUGHT TO MARRIAGE BY BRIDE

8. ATBOEGAS = 8. _____
   VANDALIZE

9. HNGETCICRO = 9. _____
   NEEDLEWORK SIMILAR TO KNITTING

10. TMECPTON = 10. _____
    DISGUST; DISTASTE

11. EIURPMSIO = 11. _____
    DOMINEERING; OVERBEARING

12. LDOMHUOS = 12. _____
    CRIMINALS; HOOLIGANS

13. ABTSHAB = 13. _____
    HOLY DAY

14. CRASIAATYLSCL = 14. _____
    IN A CUTTING MANNER

15. AIRICTNTE = 15. _____
    DETAILED

Number the Stars Vocabulary Juggle Letters 1 Answer Key

1. KANLY = 1. LANKY
LEAN; THIN

2. UUIOYSBDL = 2. DUBIOUSLY
DOUBTFULLY

3. DRIDBEEOMER = 3. EMBROIDERED
DECORATED WITH NEEDLEWORK

4. ESDLRNTEAII = 4. RESIDENTIAL
AREA WHERE HOMES ARE LOCATED

5. DESMERBUG = 5. SUBMERGED
PLUNGED UNDERWATER

6. HITEPADSCSITO = 6. SOPHISTICATED
CULTURED; REFINED

7. OUEURASST = 7. TROUSSEAU
ITEMS BROUGHT TO MARRIAGE BY BRIDE

8. ATBOEGAS = 8. SABOTAGE
VANDALIZE

9. HNGETCICRO = 9. CROCHETING
NEEDLEWORK SIMILAR TO KNITTING

10. TMECPTON = 10. CONTEMPT
DISGUST; DISTASTE

11. EIURPMSIO = 11. IMPERIOUS
DOMINEERING; OVERBEARING

12. LDOMHUOS = 12. HOODLUMS
CRIMINALS; HOOLIGANS

13. ABTSHAB = 13. SABBATH
HOLY DAY

14. CRASIAATYLSCL = 14. SARCASTICALLY
IN A CUTTING MANNER

15. AIRICTNTE = 15. INTRICATE
DETAILED

Number the Stars Vocabulary Juggle Letters 2

1. STNAOTBIE = 1. _____
   STUBBORN

2. RETDGDU = 2. _____
   PLODDED; MARCHED

3. UALGHIHTY = 3. _____
   ARROGANTLY; HIGH AND MIGHTILY

4. DSERBGUME = 4. _____
   PLUNGED UNDERWATER

5. EGONAGYUS = 5. _____
   JEWISH CHURCH

6. ETRAISIENDL = 6. _____
   AREA WHERE HOMES ARE LOCATED

7. TEBSAAGO = 7. _____
   VANDALIZE

8. NTDENIO = 8. _____
   RECITED; SPOKE

9. ENPTMCTO = 9. _____
   DISGUST; DISTASTE

10. RISOPEUIM =10. _____
    DOMINEERING; OVERBEARING

11. LITDEFNAY =11. _____
    BOLDLY; REBELLIOUSLY

12. DSXEATAERPE =12. _____
    ANNOYED; IRRITATED

13. ETITRAICN =13. _____
    DETAILED

14. DUFYLDAISINL =14. _____
    SCORNFULLY

15. NIWVAGEUNR =15. _____
    STABLE; STEADY

Number the Stars Vocabulary Juggle Letters 2 Answer Key

1. STNAOTBIE = 1. OBSTINATE
   STUBBORN

2. RETDGDU = 2. TRUDGED
   PLODDED; MARCHED

3. UALGHIHTY = 3. HAUGHTILY
   ARROGANTLY; HIGH AND MIGHTILY

4. DSERBGUME = 4. SUBMERGED
   PLUNGED UNDERWATER

5. EGONAGYUS = 5. SYNAGOGUE
   JEWISH CHURCH

6. ETRAISIENDL = 6. RESIDENTIAL
   AREA WHERE HOMES ARE LOCATED

7. TEBSAAGO = 7. SABOTAGE
   VANDALIZE

8. NTDENIO = 8. INTONED
   RECITED; SPOKE

9. ENPTMCTO = 9. CONTEMPT
   DISGUST; DISTASTE

10. RISOPEUIM =10. IMPERIOUS
    DOMINEERING; OVERBEARING

11. LITDEFNAY =11. DEFIANTLY
    BOLDLY; REBELLIOUSLY

12. DSXEATAERPE =12. EXASPERATED
    ANNOYED; IRRITATED

13. ETITRAICN =13. INTRICATE
    DETAILED

14. DUFYLDAISINL =14. DISDAINFULLY
    SCORNFULLY

15. NIWVAGEUNR =15. UNWAVERING
    STABLE; STEADY

Number the Stars Vocabulary Juggle Letters 3

1. AASGBETO = 1. _____
   VANDALIZE

2. ITNTIACER = 2. _____
   DETAILED

3. MTPEDIRNI = 3. _____
   PRESSED INTO

4. ALCRSAAYISTCL = 4. _____
   IN A CUTTING MANNER

5. AOUYSNEGG = 5. _____
   JEWISH CHURCH

6. BUSIYULOD = 6. _____
   DOUBTFULLY

7. BAIBR = 7. _____
   JEWISH MINISTER

8. STPDEIACSITOH = 8. _____
   CULTURED; REFINED

9. RUSUAOTSE = 9. _____
   ITEMS BROUGHT TO MARRIAGE BY BRIDE

10. ERDIANSLITE = 10. _____
    AREA WHERE HOMES ARE LOCATED

11. OTPMNCET = 11. _____
    DISGUST; DISTASTE

12. RSEPUMOII = 12. _____
    DOMINEERING; OVERBEARING

13. HTNERCCGOI = 13. _____
    NEEDLEWORK SIMILAR TO KNITTING

14. NSBOITTEA = 14. _____
    STUBBORN

15. RUIEANNVGW = 15. _____
    STABLE; STEADY

Number the Stars Vocabulary Juggle Letters 3 Answer Key

1. AASGBETO = 1. SABOTAGE
   VANDALIZE
2. ITNTIACER = 2. INTRICATE
   DETAILED
3. MTPEDIRNI = 3. IMPRINTED
   PRESSED INTO
4. ALCRSAAYISTCL = 4. SARCASTICALLY
   IN A CUTTING MANNER
5. AOUYSNEGG = 5. SYNAGOGUE
   JEWISH CHURCH
6. BUSIYULOD = 6. DUBIOUSLY
   DOUBTFULLY
7. BAIBR = 7. RABBI
   JEWISH MINISTER
8. STPDEIACSITOH = 8. SOPHISTICATED
   CULTURED; REFINED
9. RUSUAOTSE = 9. TROUSSEAU
   ITEMS BROUGHT TO MARRIAGE BY BRIDE
10. ERDIANSLITE =10. RESIDENTIAL
    AREA WHERE HOMES ARE LOCATED
11. OTPMNCET =11. CONTEMPT
    DISGUST; DISTASTE
12. RSEPUMOII =12. IMPERIOUS
    DOMINEERING; OVERBEARING
13. HTNERCCGOI =13. CROCHETING
    NEEDLEWORK SIMILAR TO KNITTING
14. NSBOITTEA =14. OBSTINATE
    STUBBORN
15. RUIEANNVGW =15. UNWAVERING
    STABLE; STEADY

Number the Stars Vocabulary Juggle Letters 4

1. RDIMRBODEEE = 1. _____
   DECORATED WITH NEEDLEWORK

2. EIMSPIOUR = 2. _____
   DOMINEERING; OVERBEARING

3. ENTDEGDASI = 3. _____
   APPOINTED

4. MRPNTDIIE = 4. _____
   PRESSED INTO

5. EUSOSTUAR = 5. _____
   ITEMS BROUGHT TO MARRIAGE BY BRIDE

6. SISPHDITCAETO = 6. _____
   CULTURED; REFINED

7. LYLERTILNEBGE = 7. _____
   IN A HOSTILE MANNER

8. OGSATEAB = 8. _____
   VANDALIZE

9. AEOYGNSGU = 9. _____
   JEWISH CHURCH

10. INTDFALEY =10. _____
    BOLDLY; REBELLIOUSLY

11. LHGUYITHA =11. _____
    ARROGANTLY; HIGH AND MIGHTILY

12. NCTGIHEORC =12. _____
    NEEDLEWORK SIMILAR TO KNITTING

13. DSLOUOHM =13. _____
    CRIMINALS; HOOLIGANS

14. IILDSDUFNYLA =14. _____
    SCORNFULLY

15. NATTRIEIC =15. _____
    DETAILED

Number the Stars Vocabulary Juggle Letters 4 Answer Key

1. RDIMRBODEEE = 1. EMBROIDERED
   DECORATED WITH NEEDLEWORK

2. EIMSPIOUR = 2. IMPERIOUS
   DOMINEERING; OVERBEARING

3. ENTDEGDASI = 3. DESIGNATED
   APPOINTED

4. MRPNTDIIE = 4. IMPRINTED
   PRESSED INTO

5. EUSOSTUAR = 5. TROUSSEAU
   ITEMS BROUGHT TO MARRIAGE BY BRIDE

6. SISPHDITCAETO = 6. SOPHISTICATED
   CULTURED; REFINED

7. LYLERTILNEBGE = 7. BELLIGERENTLY
   IN A HOSTILE MANNER

8. OGSATEAB = 8. SABOTAGE
   VANDALIZE

9. AEOYGNSGU = 9. SYNAGOGUE
   JEWISH CHURCH

10. INTDFALEY =10. DEFIANTLY
    BOLDLY; REBELLIOUSLY

11. LHGUYITHA =11. HAUGHTILY
    ARROGANTLY; HIGH AND MIGHTILY

12. NCTGIHEORC =12. CROCHETING
    NEEDLEWORK SIMILAR TO KNITTING

13. DSLOUOHM =13. HOODLUMS
    CRIMINALS; HOOLIGANS

14. IILDSDUFNYLA =14. DISDAINFULLY
    SCORNFULLY

15. NATTRIEIC =15. INTRICATE
    DETAILED

BELLIGERENTLY	IN A HOSTILE MANNER
CONTEMPT	DISGUST; DISTASTE
CROCHETING	NEEDLEWORK SIMILAR TO KNITTING
DEFIANTLY	BOLDLY; REBELLIOUSLY
DESIGNATED	APPOINTED
DISDAINFULLY	SCORNFULLY

DUBIOUSLY	DOUBTFULLY
EMBROIDERED	DECORATED WITH NEEDLEWORK
EXASPERATED	ANNOYED; IRRITATED
HAUGHTILY	ARROGANTLY; HIGH AND MIGHTILY
HOODLUMS	CRIMINALS; HOOLIGANS
IMPASSIVE	UNEMOTIONAL; INDIFFERENT

IMPERIOUS	DOMINEERING; OVERBEARING
IMPRINTED	PRESSED INTO
INTONED	RECITED; SPOKE
INTRICATE	DETAILED
LANKY	LEAN; THIN
OBSTINATE	STUBBORN

RABBI	JEWISH MINISTER
RESIDENTIAL	AREA WHERE HOMES ARE LOCATED
SABBATH	HOLY DAY
SABOTAGE	VANDALIZE
SARCASTICALLY	IN A CUTTING MANNER
SOPHISTICATED	CULTURED; REFINED

SUBMERGED	PLUNGED UNDERWATER
SYNAGOGUE	JEWISH CHURCH
TROUSSEAU	ITEMS BROUGHT TO MARRIAGE BY BRIDE
TRUDGED	PLODDED; MARCHED
UNWAVERING	STABLE; STEADY

Number the Stars Vocabulary

CONTEMPT	DESIGNATED	DISDAINFULLY	SUBMERGED	SARCASTICALLY
SOPHISTICATED	TRUDGED	INTONED	OBSTINATE	SYNAGOGUE
IMPERIOUS	TROUSSEAU	FREE SPACE	DUBIOUSLY	IMPRINTED
LANKY	DEFIANTLY	SABOTAGE	RESIDENTIAL	HOODLUMS
IMPASSIVE	BELLIGERENTLY	CROCHETING	EMBROIDERED	SABBATH

Number the Stars Vocabulary

EXASPERATED	HAUGHTILY	UNWAVERING	INTRICATE	SABBATH
EMBROIDERED	CROCHETING	BELLIGERENTLY	IMPASSIVE	HOODLUMS
RESIDENTIAL	SABOTAGE	FREE SPACE	LANKY	IMPRINTED
DUBIOUSLY	RABBI	TROUSSEAU	IMPERIOUS	SYNAGOGUE
OBSTINATE	INTONED	TRUDGED	SOPHISTICATED	SARCASTICALLY

Number the Stars Vocabulary

INTRICATE	INTONED	DUBIOUSLY	UNWAVERING	IMPASSIVE
CONTEMPT	SABOTAGE	CROCHETING	HAUGHTILY	SUBMERGED
DISDAINFULLY	DESIGNATED	FREE SPACE	EXASPERATED	IMPERIOUS
SOPHISTICATED	DEFIANTLY	RABBI	HOODLUMS	EMBROIDERED
SARCASTICALLY	TRUDGED	LANKY	SYNAGOGUE	IMPRINTED

Number the Stars Vocabulary

TROUSSEAU	OBSTINATE	BELLIGERENTLY	SABBATH	IMPRINTED
SYNAGOGUE	LANKY	TRUDGED	SARCASTICALLY	EMBROIDERED
HOODLUMS	RABBI	FREE SPACE	SOPHISTICATED	IMPERIOUS
EXASPERATED	RESIDENTIAL	DESIGNATED	DISDAINFULLY	SUBMERGED
HAUGHTILY	CROCHETING	SABOTAGE	CONTEMPT	IMPASSIVE

Number the Stars Vocabulary

SABOTAGE	OBSTINATE	UNWAVERING	RABBI	IMPRINTED
EMBROIDERED	INTONED	DEFIANTLY	SARCASTICALLY	IMPASSIVE
SYNAGOGUE	DESIGNATED	FREE SPACE	HAUGHTILY	TRUDGED
DISDAINFULLY	TROUSSEAU	HOODLUMS	EXASPERATED	RESIDENTIAL
CROCHETING	DUBIOUSLY	SABBATH	BELLIGERENTLY	LANKY

Number the Stars Vocabulary

CONTEMPT	SUBMERGED	IMPERIOUS	SOPHISTICATED	LANKY
BELLIGERENTLY	SABBATH	DUBIOUSLY	CROCHETING	RESIDENTIAL
EXASPERATED	HOODLUMS	FREE SPACE	DISDAINFULLY	TRUDGED
HAUGHTILY	INTRICATE	DESIGNATED	SYNAGOGUE	IMPASSIVE
SARCASTICALLY	DEFIANTLY	INTONED	EMBROIDERED	IMPRINTED

Number the Stars Vocabulary

BELLIGERENTLY	INTONED	DESIGNATED	DEFIANTLY	SUBMERGED
SYNAGOGUE	HAUGHTILY	EMBROIDERED	OBSTINATE	EXASPERATED
SABOTAGE	DISDAINFULLY	FREE SPACE	IMPASSIVE	SARCASTICALLY
RABBI	IMPRINTED	RESIDENTIAL	LANKY	DUBIOUSLY
UNWAVERING	HOODLUMS	TROUSSEAU	IMPERIOUS	TRUDGED

Number the Stars Vocabulary

SOPHISTICATED	SABBATH	CONTEMPT	CROCHETING	TRUDGED
IMPERIOUS	TROUSSEAU	HOODLUMS	UNWAVERING	DUBIOUSLY
LANKY	RESIDENTIAL	FREE SPACE	RABBI	SARCASTICALLY
IMPASSIVE	INTRICATE	DISDAINFULLY	SABOTAGE	EXASPERATED
OBSTINATE	EMBROIDERED	HAUGHTILY	SYNAGOGUE	SUBMERGED

Number the Stars Vocabulary

TROUSSEAU	INTRICATE	UNWAVERING	HAUGHTILY	RABBI
IMPERIOUS	TRUDGED	DEFIANTLY	IMPRINTED	SARCASTICALLY
INTONED	OBSTINATE	FREE SPACE	CROCHETING	SABOTAGE
SUBMERGED	DISDAINFULLY	SABBATH	CONTEMPT	SYNAGOGUE
SOPHISTICATED	IMPASSIVE	LANKY	DESIGNATED	HOODLUMS

Number the Stars Vocabulary

BELLIGERENTLY	EXASPERATED	DUBIOUSLY	EMBROIDERED	HOODLUMS
DESIGNATED	LANKY	IMPASSIVE	SOPHISTICATED	SYNAGOGUE
CONTEMPT	SABBATH	FREE SPACE	SUBMERGED	SABOTAGE
CROCHETING	RESIDENTIAL	OBSTINATE	INTONED	SARCASTICALLY
IMPRINTED	DEFIANTLY	TRUDGED	IMPERIOUS	RABBI

Number the Stars Vocabulary

IMPERIOUS	INTONED	IMPASSIVE	RABBI	OBSTINATE
SABBATH	SARCASTICALLY	SOPHISTICATED	CONTEMPT	DEFIANTLY
HAUGHTILY	DESIGNATED	FREE SPACE	DUBIOUSLY	IMPRINTED
LANKY	TROUSSEAU	BELLIGERENTLY	INTRICATE	CROCHETING
SABOTAGE	SYNAGOGUE	SUBMERGED	HOODLUMS	TRUDGED

Number the Stars Vocabulary

EXASPERATED	EMBROIDERED	RESIDENTIAL	UNWAVERING	TRUDGED
HOODLUMS	SUBMERGED	SYNAGOGUE	SABOTAGE	CROCHETING
INTRICATE	BELLIGERENTLY	FREE SPACE	LANKY	IMPRINTED
DUBIOUSLY	DISDAINFULLY	DESIGNATED	HAUGHTILY	DEFIANTLY
CONTEMPT	SOPHISTICATED	SARCASTICALLY	SABBATH	OBSTINATE

Number the Stars Vocabulary

RESIDENTIAL	DUBIOUSLY	DEFIANTLY	DISDAINFULLY	LANKY
TRUDGED	CROCHETING	IMPASSIVE	CONTEMPT	HAUGHTILY
DESIGNATED	SARCASTICALLY	FREE SPACE	EXASPERATED	SABBATH
TROUSSEAU	IMPRINTED	SYNAGOGUE	IMPERIOUS	INTRICATE
SABOTAGE	RABBI	EMBROIDERED	SUBMERGED	INTONED

Number the Stars Vocabulary

SOPHISTICATED	BELLIGERENTLY	HOODLUMS	UNWAVERING	INTONED
SUBMERGED	EMBROIDERED	RABBI	SABOTAGE	INTRICATE
IMPERIOUS	SYNAGOGUE	FREE SPACE	TROUSSEAU	SABBATH
EXASPERATED	OBSTINATE	SARCASTICALLY	DESIGNATED	HAUGHTILY
CONTEMPT	IMPASSIVE	CROCHETING	TRUDGED	LANKY

Number the Stars Vocabulary

IMPRINTED	SABOTAGE	RABBI	IMPERIOUS	LANKY
CONTEMPT	EMBROIDERED	DISDAINFULLY	OBSTINATE	SABBATH
EXASPERATED	INTONED	FREE SPACE	SUBMERGED	TROUSSEAU
DESIGNATED	BELLIGERENTLY	CROCHETING	DEFIANTLY	UNWAVERING
HAUGHTILY	DUBIOUSLY	SOPHISTICATED	IMPASSIVE	HOODLUMS

Number the Stars Vocabulary

SYNAGOGUE	INTRICATE	TRUDGED	SARCASTICALLY	HOODLUMS
IMPASSIVE	SOPHISTICATED	DUBIOUSLY	HAUGHTILY	UNWAVERING
DEFIANTLY	CROCHETING	FREE SPACE	DESIGNATED	TROUSSEAU
SUBMERGED	RESIDENTIAL	INTONED	EXASPERATED	SABBATH
OBSTINATE	DISDAINFULLY	EMBROIDERED	CONTEMPT	LANKY

Number the Stars Vocabulary

TRUDGED	IMPASSIVE	IMPRINTED	SYNAGOGUE	RESIDENTIAL
DESIGNATED	HAUGHTILY	HOODLUMS	TROUSSEAU	OBSTINATE
BELLIGERENTLY	INTONED	FREE SPACE	LANKY	RABBI
SUBMERGED	EMBROIDERED	UNWAVERING	DUBIOUSLY	SARCASTICALLY
INTRICATE	IMPERIOUS	CROCHETING	DISDAINFULLY	SABOTAGE

Number the Stars Vocabulary

SOPHISTICATED	DEFIANTLY	EXASPERATED	SABBATH	SABOTAGE
DISDAINFULLY	CROCHETING	IMPERIOUS	INTRICATE	SARCASTICALLY
DUBIOUSLY	UNWAVERING	FREE SPACE	SUBMERGED	RABBI
LANKY	CONTEMPT	INTONED	BELLIGERENTLY	OBSTINATE
TROUSSEAU	HOODLUMS	HAUGHTILY	DESIGNATED	RESIDENTIAL

Number the Stars Vocabulary

DISDAINFULLY	EXASPERATED	SUBMERGED	DEFIANTLY	BELLIGERENTLY
TROUSSEAU	CROCHETING	INTRICATE	SYNAGOGUE	EMBROIDERED
SARCASTICALLY	SABOTAGE	FREE SPACE	TRUDGED	HOODLUMS
IMPRINTED	CONTEMPT	LANKY	RESIDENTIAL	DESIGNATED
RABBI	DUBIOUSLY	HAUGHTILY	OBSTINATE	IMPASSIVE

Number the Stars Vocabulary

UNWAVERING	SOPHISTICATED	IMPERIOUS	INTONED	IMPASSIVE
OBSTINATE	HAUGHTILY	DUBIOUSLY	RABBI	DESIGNATED
RESIDENTIAL	LANKY	FREE SPACE	IMPRINTED	HOODLUMS
TRUDGED	SABBATH	SABOTAGE	SARCASTICALLY	EMBROIDERED
SYNAGOGUE	INTRICATE	CROCHETING	TROUSSEAU	BELLIGERENTLY

Number the Stars Vocabulary

TRUDGED	RESIDENTIAL	IMPASSIVE	SYNAGOGUE	INTONED
SABBATH	DEFIANTLY	SARCASTICALLY	SABOTAGE	IMPRINTED
OBSTINATE	SUBMERGED	FREE SPACE	EXASPERATED	LANKY
INTRICATE	DUBIOUSLY	BELLIGERENTLY	HAUGHTILY	CROCHETING
HOODLUMS	UNWAVERING	DESIGNATED	TROUSSEAU	EMBROIDERED

Number the Stars Vocabulary

CONTEMPT	RABBI	SOPHISTICATED	DISDAINFULLY	EMBROIDERED
TROUSSEAU	DESIGNATED	UNWAVERING	HOODLUMS	CROCHETING
HAUGHTILY	BELLIGERENTLY	FREE SPACE	INTRICATE	LANKY
EXASPERATED	IMPERIOUS	SUBMERGED	OBSTINATE	IMPRINTED
SABOTAGE	SARCASTICALLY	DEFIANTLY	SABBATH	INTONED

Number the Stars Vocabulary

CONTEMPT	RESIDENTIAL	UNWAVERING	BELLIGERENTLY	SYNAGOGUE
EXASPERATED	DESIGNATED	IMPASSIVE	SARCASTICALLY	IMPERIOUS
SUBMERGED	INTRICATE	FREE SPACE	TROUSSEAU	SABOTAGE
LANKY	CROCHETING	HOODLUMS	IMPRINTED	SOPHISTICATED
RABBI	OBSTINATE	DISDAINFULLY	DUBIOUSLY	HAUGHTILY

Number the Stars Vocabulary

TRUDGED	EMBROIDERED	DEFIANTLY	INTONED	HAUGHTILY
DUBIOUSLY	DISDAINFULLY	OBSTINATE	RABBI	SOPHISTICATED
IMPRINTED	HOODLUMS	FREE SPACE	LANKY	SABOTAGE
TROUSSEAU	SABBATH	INTRICATE	SUBMERGED	IMPERIOUS
SARCASTICALLY	IMPASSIVE	DESIGNATED	EXASPERATED	SYNAGOGUE

Number the Stars Vocabulary

SYNAGOGUE	HAUGHTILY	RESIDENTIAL	IMPRINTED	TROUSSEAU
CROCHETING	SABBATH	LANKY	OBSTINATE	DISDAINFULLY
SOPHISTICATED	DUBIOUSLY	FREE SPACE	IMPERIOUS	IMPASSIVE
INTONED	CONTEMPT	HOODLUMS	INTRICATE	RABBI
TRUDGED	EMBROIDERED	SUBMERGED	EXASPERATED	SARCASTICALLY

Number the Stars Vocabulary

BELLIGERENTLY	UNWAVERING	SABOTAGE	DESIGNATED	SARCASTICALLY
EXASPERATED	SUBMERGED	EMBROIDERED	TRUDGED	RABBI
INTRICATE	HOODLUMS	FREE SPACE	INTONED	IMPASSIVE
IMPERIOUS	DEFIANTLY	DUBIOUSLY	SOPHISTICATED	DISDAINFULLY
OBSTINATE	LANKY	SABBATH	CROCHETING	TROUSSEAU

Number the Stars Vocabulary

DISDAINFULLY	TRUDGED	SYNAGOGUE	CONTEMPT	HOODLUMS
IMPRINTED	DUBIOUSLY	BELLIGERENTLY	IMPASSIVE	HAUGHTILY
TROUSSEAU	CROCHETING	FREE SPACE	EXASPERATED	SABBATH
DESIGNATED	UNWAVERING	INTRICATE	SUBMERGED	SABOTAGE
OBSTINATE	RESIDENTIAL	IMPERIOUS	RABBI	SOPHISTICATED

Number the Stars Vocabulary

EMBROIDERED	SARCASTICALLY	INTONED	LANKY	SOPHISTICATED
RABBI	IMPERIOUS	RESIDENTIAL	OBSTINATE	SABOTAGE
SUBMERGED	INTRICATE	FREE SPACE	DESIGNATED	SABBATH
EXASPERATED	DEFIANTLY	CROCHETING	TROUSSEAU	HAUGHTILY
IMPASSIVE	BELLIGERENTLY	DUBIOUSLY	IMPRINTED	HOODLUMS

Number the Stars Vocabulary

OBSTINATE	TROUSSEAU	IMPERIOUS	SARCASTICALLY	EXASPERATED
DUBIOUSLY	HAUGHTILY	UNWAVERING	CROCHETING	IMPRINTED
CONTEMPT	INTONED	FREE SPACE	SYNAGOGUE	SUBMERGED
SABBATH	RABBI	RESIDENTIAL	DESIGNATED	DISDAINFULLY
HOODLUMS	EMBROIDERED	SOPHISTICATED	SABOTAGE	LANKY

Number the Stars Vocabulary

INTRICATE	IMPASSIVE	DEFIANTLY	BELLIGERENTLY	LANKY
SABOTAGE	SOPHISTICATED	EMBROIDERED	HOODLUMS	DISDAINFULLY
DESIGNATED	RESIDENTIAL	FREE SPACE	SABBATH	SUBMERGED
SYNAGOGUE	TRUDGED	INTONED	CONTEMPT	IMPRINTED
CROCHETING	UNWAVERING	HAUGHTILY	DUBIOUSLY	EXASPERATED

Number the Stars Vocabulary

UNWAVERING	SYNAGOGUE	IMPASSIVE	TRUDGED	RABBI
HAUGHTILY	DESIGNATED	LANKY	SARCASTICALLY	CONTEMPT
SABOTAGE	CROCHETING	FREE SPACE	INTONED	BELLIGERENTLY
SOPHISTICATED	IMPRINTED	SABBATH	INTRICATE	HOODLUMS
RESIDENTIAL	SUBMERGED	OBSTINATE	TROUSSEAU	IMPERIOUS

Number the Stars Vocabulary

EMBROIDERED	EXASPERATED	DUBIOUSLY	DISDAINFULLY	IMPERIOUS
TROUSSEAU	OBSTINATE	SUBMERGED	RESIDENTIAL	HOODLUMS
INTRICATE	SABBATH	FREE SPACE	SOPHISTICATED	BELLIGERENTLY
INTONED	DEFIANTLY	CROCHETING	SABOTAGE	CONTEMPT
SARCASTICALLY	LANKY	DESIGNATED	HAUGHTILY	RABBI